W9-AYC-622

THE MOON
Steppingstone to Outer Space

523.3
Shuttlesworth

THE MOON

Steppingstone to Outer Space

DOROTHY E. SHUTTLESWORTH

AND

LEE ANN WILLIAMS

Doubleday & Company, Inc.

Garden City, New York

1977

MADISON JHS LIBRARY
TRUMBULL, CONN.

Library of Congress Cataloging in Publication Data

Shuttlesworth, Dorothy Edwards, 1907–
The moon, steppingstone to outer space.

Includes index.
SUMMARY: Discusses theories of the moon's
origin, its physical characteristics, and space
programs that have made lunar exploration possible.
1. Moon—Juvenile literature. [1. Moon]
I. Williams, Lee Ann, joint author. II. Title.
QB582.S54   523.3
ISBN 0-385-12118-0 Trade
0-385-12119-9 Prebound
Library of Congress Catalog Card Number 76–50787

Copyright © 1977 by Dorothy E. Shuttlesworth and Lee Ann Williams
Printed in the United States of America
All Rights Reserved
First Edition

All photos in this book are through the courtesy of the National Aeronautics
and Space Administration, with the following exceptions:
American Museum of Natural History, pp. 8, 12, 24, 62 (left), 73, 76,
77, 80, 83, 88, 91.
James M. Staples, p. 4.
Wide World Photos, p. 85.

For Our JAMES GREGORY
with love and great expectations

Contents

THE MOON
Steppingstone to Outer Space

1

What Is a Moon?

How can anything be so well known as the moon, yet still be mysterious! "Our" moon—the moon that shines on the earth—has been seen by people for millions of years, and for much of that time it was looked at with awe, with reverence, and often with fear. Then came a period when it was carefully examined through telescopes and in photographs made by cameras sent to outer space. And as knowledge increased, hope grew ever stronger that some day people could land on its strangely exciting surface and explore it.

In 1969 that is exactly what happened.

Yet in spite of all that has been learned, there are still unanswered questions about the creation of our moon and the origin of others—that is, natural satellites that revolve around other planets. Altogether thirty-four moons are known to exist. Mars has two; Jupiter, fourteen; Saturn, ten; Neptune, five; Uranus, two. All but the earth's moon have been given names. Ours remains simply "the" moon.

Until 1610, when Galileo used his telescope, no one suspected the existence of any moon besides the one that orbits the earth. But one bright night when this pioneer astronomer put his new invention to use, he was amazed to see four moons orbiting Jupiter. In later years, as telescopes were improved and became increasingly powerful, more and more moons came into focus. The thirty-fourth was discovered as recently as 1975.

By means of more sophisticated instruments, a variety of discoveries were made about these far-distant moons. Then came the spectacular breakthrough in outer space studies when astronauts landed on the moon, explored it, pictured it, and returned safely to earth.

It might seem that as a result of their incredible moon journeys all questions could at last be settled. But many answers still lie in the future as rocks and soil brought back are analyzed, thousands of photographs are carefully studied, and experts ponder information given them by seismometers set up on the moon.

You may sense the changing opinions about the moon if you compare definitions appearing in some dictionaries and encyclopedias with current articles and books. A dictionary may state that the moon is "a huge ball of gray rock which is a satellite of the earth." Then you may see in a magazine article that the moon is called a planet. And what is a planet? A dictionary may say, "any of the nine largest objects that travel around the sun." This obviously is leaving out the moon.

However, due to research made possible through NASA (the National Aeronautics and Space Administration) the moon is now considered a small planet—having a core, a rocky mantle, and a crust. So, because it circles around the earth, we may call it our planet-satellite.

But in spite of all the discoveries made in recent years, scientists are still pondering mysteries concerning the moon's origin. They are also looking ahead to new explorations that could take earth people to Mars and other

Brought back from the moon! A two-pound rock collected by the first men to reach the moon—astronauts of the Apollo 11 mission—on exhibit at the Smithsonian Institution. It was guarded as carefully as a rare diamond would be, and it created even more interest.

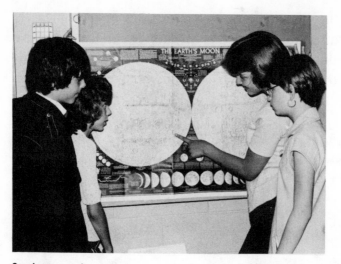

Students study a moon map to locate areas explored by astronauts . . .

And they look forward to the possibility of making themselves at home on the moon when it is being used for scientific work and as a launching site for travel to other planets.

planets. And in their thinking, the moon begins to play a new role in the activities of mankind. It is seen as a working base for the coming Space Age.

Not only scientists are involved with thoughts about our future with the moon and outer space. Girls and boys studying astronomy find themselves challenged, as when NASA conducted a Skylab Student Project. This was a contest for students in secondary schools to suggest experiments that could be carried out on Skylab missions. Twenty-five were selected for use. Another contest was for an emblem to be used for the Viking-Mars program. Of the many designs submitted from all over the United States, one was selected and is being used as the official Viking insignia.

It is not likely that the moon will quickly become a giant workshop for space travel as planning turns more and more to distant planets. But laboratories may be set up on the moon where technicians could work for a month or more at a stretch. Later a colony might develop where people could stay as long as a year, having well-organized commuting between moon and earth.

Does such a development seem too imaginative to be taken seriously? It does not if we look back less than fifty years and realize that so short a time ago a trip to the moon seemed an impossible dream to almost everyone. Now not only have men walked on the moon, but people on earth have watched them there by means of television. Fifty years from now, what dreams of today will have become realities! These dreams become especially fascinating when they are compared with moon myths and legends that were accepted as fact for countless years.

2
Myths, Legends, and a Hoax

Perhaps some evening you will be looking at a bright moon and see that clouds are coming near it. The clouds move closer, and suddenly the moon disappears behind them. At the sudden darkening of the sky you may think, "The weather is changing. We'll probably have rain tomorrow." You surely would not say, "Dragons have swallowed the moon!"

In ancient China, however, that idea would have been accepted as perfectly reasonable. In artwork of the time, clouds often were turned into traditional dragons, and the moon sometimes was shown between two of them—about to be devoured. Because there usually was a need for rain, and clouds did, many times, cover the moon before rain started, farmers and shepherds rejoiced at this action of the "dragons." And so a myth about helpful dragons swallowing the moon became established.

As a turn-about tale concerning who ate what in the heavens, there was a belief that a full moon ate clouds.

And the Cherokee Indians blamed a lunar eclipse on a huge frog that nibbled at the edge of the moon. By screaming, beating kettles, ringing bells, and otherwise setting up a great din, the Indians frightened the frog away, thus saving the moon.

American Indian tribes varied in a number of ways, but all were rich in myths and legends, many of which concerned the world of nature. Very often the moon was involved. One Iroquois explanation of the universe told of a good spirit who created the sun and daylight while a bad spirit was responsible for the night. However, the good spirit then offset total darkness by creating the moon and stars.

A legend of the Blackfoot tribe told of a man who was trying to escape from his wife and, being unsuccessful on earth, jumped into the sky, where he became the sun. His wife leaped after him, but she could not jump as far as he had, and she became the moon.

Among the words pictured in Indian sign language that were understood by all tribes was the "picture" for moon. And this, combined with another symbol, indicated a certain month. For the moon symbol the right hand was outstretched, palm up, with thumb and index finger curved to suggest a crescent moon. This would follow a symbol such as "snow" for January, "green grass" for April, and "falling leaf" for October. The passing of time was expressed by "many moons ago."

Today a number of superstitions concerning natural forces still exist—a great number of them being concerned with the moon. This is not surprising because of its changing appearance—from "new" to "full" each month, and its partial and total eclipses—and also because the moon has very real influence on the earth, in

Myths of the Blackfoot Indian tribe about various astronomical bodies are illustrated in this painting. The central figures represent the Sun God pursuing the Moon Goddess.

reflecting varying amounts of sunlight to our planet, and in regulating tides.

Many farmers and fishermen claim, and show apparent proof, that success with fish or crops depends on their activities being carried on when the moon is in a correct phase.

And some animals such as wolves and dogs often are compelled to howl at a bright moon. Why? There seems to be some eerie force in moonlight that affects animals. So it is understandable that the moon became associated with strange behavior in people. "Lunatics," it was believed, were those who had become crazed from association with the moon. Even today this idea may be taken seriously as so-called experts on human behavior say that exposure to bright moonlight can have an unhappy effect on people with nervous disorders.

In tracing moon myths, we find what fantastic imaginations many primitive people had. Even before dragons were making "news" in China, the Bushmen of African jungles thought the sun (which they believed to be a man) was angry with the moon, and stabbed it savagely until it was almost destroyed. But when the moon begged for mercy, the sun stopped his attack—whereupon the moon grew large and round again. Of course later, when it became full, the stabbing began anew.

Through the ages, as moon myths continued to originate and be accepted, and legends became established, some of them contradicted others. But both points of view usually continued to flourish.

In North America and England phases of the moon were carefully noted by farmers for the right planting times. Such underground vegetables as potatoes, carrots, and turnips were to be started when there was no moonlight. Above-ground crops such as corn were planted at full moon, or at least when the moon was very bright.

The moon was important also in harvesting. Even horseradish was given special attention; it was said to be most flavorful if dug at full moon. By contrast many crops were supposed to be best if harvested at the "dark of the moon." In parts of the world where a full moon in September and October is especially bright, many people call it a "harvest moon," and for years this was supposed to be a special gift from heaven to farmers. The fact is that during those two months the moon makes a smaller angle with the horizon and, as a result, is more radiant.

English farm people had countless chores regulated by the moon. Eggs must be set out for hens at the moon's increase, and that also was the time when mares should be mated, and sheep sheared to increase the bulk of their wool. When feather beds needed to be turned, the job should be done when the moon was waning. This would make the feathers lie more smoothly; a bright moon would attract them too strongly. Washdays also were influenced, because if new clothes were washed for the first time at new moon, they would not last long.

The areas that show darkly on the face of the moon resulted in a number of strange notions. In the Ojibway Indian tribe the markings were said to be the shadow of a boy carrying two water pails. The explanation for his being there was that he had disobeyed a tribal rule: No one was to look at the moon for any length of time. But the boy wanted to find out what would happen and one evening when he was carrying water pails, he kept staring at the sky. The moon came closer and closer to earth, then suddenly snatched him and carried him up into the heavens, and he never escaped. This story was told to young Ojibway children to make sure they would be cautious about moon-gazing.

In Scandinavian countries a similar fantasy has long been popular. According to this legend, the moon stole a boy and girl from the earth as they were drawing water from a well. Afterward the children, their bucket, and the pole on which they carried it could be seen silhouetted against the bright moon. Although the children in the original story were called Hjuki and Bil, these names, through the years, became Jack and Jill, and the rhyme about their going "up the hill to fetch a pail of water" became a popular nursery rhyme. The gradual disappearance of the markings on the moon as it moved from full to last quarter was translated into Jack's falling down, followed by Jill's tumble.

People have also imagined the dark regions to be a "man in the moon," a rabbit, and other figures. The truth is they are the *maria* that you will read about in Chapter 6.

Many predictions about luck have been concerned with the moon. Good luck, bad luck, and all kinds of predictions, including death, could be foreseen, it was believed, by how the moon looked or how a person happened to see it. If, for example, you saw a new moon for the first time over your left shoulder, and had a silver coin in your pocket, and turned this over while making a wish, the wish would come true.

A crescent moon has generally been considered lucky. In some regions people think the idea of a horseshoe being lucky was based on the fact that its shape is like that of a crescent moon. However, there are other beliefs about the lucky horseshoe that have nothing to do with the moon.

With all these strange notions dating back many centuries, there are some happenings of quite recent times that show people were always ready to believe the most fantastic tales about the moon. Less than a hundred and fifty years ago a hoax carried out by a newspaper writer convinced many intelligent, educated individuals that the moon was populated by bat-men and other strange creatures.

The hoax was inspired when Sir John Herschel, a prominent astronomer of the early nineteenth century, had a powerful telescope built which he took to the Cape of Good Hope. He announced that he was going to stay

THE INHABITANTS OF THE MOON,

A newspaper reporter, through dishonest scheming, gained wide publicity for himself—and the moon—by claiming that a noted astronomer (who was on an expedition and out of touch with the rest of the world) was seeing through his telescope the moon's surface and some extraordinary characters living there.

there for several years, studying the constellations of the southern hemisphere.

His plan was noted by a journalist named Richard Locke, who had left his native England for the United States to become a staff writer for *The Sun,* a New York newspaper with a wide circulation. His imagination stirred, he thought of a strictly dishonest way to gain readers' attention. He would write fantastic accounts of discoveries which Herschel was supposed to be making with his new telescope. And because the astronomer was isolated on the other side of the world, he would not learn about these stories until long after they were published;

meanwhile Richard Locke's name would become well known.

Locke wrote his series of "startling revelations." *The Sun* printed them in good faith, and *The New York Times* stated they were "possible and probable." A letter was written to him by a woman's club of Massachusetts asking for advice on the best way to get in touch with the moon people in order to convert them to their own form of religion.

Some people were dubious about the accounts, however, and two years after they began, astronomers were saying positively that the moon had no atmosphere, therefore it could not be supporting the kind of life Locke described. The great Moon Hoax was finally exposed by another newspaper, and gradually "believers" began to treat the whole thing as a joke.

Historical Theories

A theory is not mere guesswork, nor does it result from vivid imaginations as myths do. It is an explanation of a phenomenon based on actual knowledge, but lacking enough facts to make the explanation solid and unshakable.

So it came about that as scientists studied the moon through telescopes, through observing its motions, and through mathematical computation, a number of reasonable theories about its origin, make-up, and behavior were proposed. And although these are now outdated, they give fascinating evidence of man's constantly developing desire to understand the universe.

One impressive theory about the moon's creation was proposed in 1879 by mathematician George Darwin, son of the famous naturalist Charles Darwin. Scientists had long acknowledged the moon's influence on the rise and fall of tides on the earth, but Darwin was the first to make a precise study of this relationship.

Eventually he proposed that a tidal process may have resulted in the separation of the moon from the earth, at a time when the young earth was a fiery, molten body that spun on its axis much more rapidly than it does today. The sun's gravitational pull on the pliable earth, he thought, would at some point have given rise to massive tides and caused the earth to fling off a huge amount of the material that formed the tidal bulge.

Darwin's ideas, which became known as the Resonance Theory, gained many supporters during the fifty years that followed his original statement. To add credibility to the hypothesis, it was argued that the basin of the Pacific Ocean had been created by the expulsion of the material which formed the moon. And seemingly in support of this thinking, studies of rock from the Pacific Ocean floor showed that it did not consist of granite—which is the typical crustal covering of the earth. Instead it is basalt, a rock that usually lies under the granite.

Although apparently such facts are strong evidence in favor of the Resonance Theory, they cannot outweigh the points against it. For one thing, the attraction between the materials at the earth's surface would have been too great to allow the tidal bulge to separate from the earth. And any scar created in the earth (if the earth was molten at the time) would soon have healed and been closed over. Also, the gravitational pull of the earth on the freed material would have been great enough to cause it to disintegrate, forming a ring of dust and fine particles around the earth. This obviously never happened.

A later theory that still reflected some of Darwin's ideas was developed by an American astronomer, Gerard P. Kuiper, in 1915. He suggested that the solar system began as a saucer-shaped cloud of gas and dust, and as this disk rotated around the primitive sun, it began to break up and then form into solid particles. Some of these particles began colliding and then often would cling together. This process would be repeated with the enlarged particles and, as more and more of them merged, the early planets were formed.

These young planets supposedly were much larger than the planets are today because, as the force of gravity pulled closer together the materials of which each was formed, they shrank. This condensation caused them to rotate with ever-increasing speed, and as they spun, some of their mass may have been cast off. Such an expelled mass may have formed a moon.

Like Darwin's theory, this one has its flaws. Lunar samples brought back by the Apollo astronauts show the moon to be very different chemically from the earth. For example, where the moon is rich in uranium, the earth is poor. On the other hand, the earth has abundant iron, gold, and potassium, while these elements seemingly are scarce on the moon. If the earth and its moon were formed together in the manner Kuiper describes, why should they differ so widely in chemical content?

Located between the planets Mars and Jupiter is an area called the "asteroid belt." The asteroids found there range in size from a few miles to five hundred miles in diameter. A number of astronomers believe these may account for some of Jupiter's and Saturn's moons. Their theory states that if such is the case, it could be that the earth's moon is a captured asteroid.

Other scientists suggest it might have been a small planet formed near Mercury, and that the moon originally had its own path around the sun. Then, the theory further states, at some point Mercury's gravitation might have bumped the moon out of this orbit, sending it close to the earth—close enough, in fact, to be captured by our own planet.

However, in order to come under the earth's gravitational hold, the moon would have had to come very close indeed—so close that the earth's pull would have caused huge land tides on the moon. Such tidal forces would probably have pulled the moon apart, so that it would have turned into a Saturn-like ring encircling the earth rather than remaining a solid sphere.

If the moon was not a space wanderer captured by the earth, nor an offspring, literally torn out of the earth's body, what was its origin?

The most recent theory, as presented at the Fifth Lunar Science Conference held in Houston, Texas, in 1974, is to some extent a form of the capture theory. However, it differs in one very important area. It suggests that the moon was captured a piece at a time—not in one fell swoop. Tiny "moonlets" crashed into each other until eventually the moon, as we know it today, was formed.

This theory is based on studies of the lunar rocks brought back by the Apollo astronauts. But although there are hundreds of pounds of these samples, they represent only a relatively small portion of the moon. Can we be certain, then, that other areas might not give different information? With all the hard evidence that has now been assembled, we are still seeking a final answer. And although this long delay in being sure may seem strange, we must remember that the origin of the earth itself, which scientists have been studying for centuries, still is a riddle.

4

Shooting for the Moon

By the beginning of the twentieth century, improved tele-scopes and observatories were making studies of the moon from the earth increasingly efficient. Yet inquiring minds were not satisfied with observations from a distance of about a quarter of a million miles. People wished for some way to travel to this ever-intriguing satellite.

About that time science-fiction writers such as Jules Verne and H. G. Wells encouraged this kind of thinking. Books bearing the titles *The First Men in the Moon* and *From the Earth to the Moon* were among their most pop-ular. Although these two men were not scientists, they proposed some extremely intelligent ideas for space travel. One fantasy used a space-gun for sending a projectile be-tween earth and moon—a device very close to the workable one of rocket propulsion. Another touched on solving the problems of weightlessness and gravity in outer space.

Fictional inventions were exciting to read about, but they did not, in truth, bring people any closer to success with a real moon expedition. It was in 1926 that Robert H. Goddard, a hard-working professor whose particular interest was in rockets, contributed a definite step toward that goal. He did so by making a change from the solid propellants that had commonly been used to ignite a rocket engine to liquid fuel.

On March 16 of that year Professor Goddard took a home-made rocket to a snow-covered field near his home in Massachusetts and lit the blowlamp he had fastened under it. The rocket took off, and although the liquid propellants kept it going for only a few seconds, it reached a height of 184 feet, traveling at a speed of sixty miles an hour. With this modest beginning a new day dawned for rocketry. Forty years later liquid-propellant rockets were to make possible a space age more breathtaking than fiction had been.

Unhappily, for a number of years after Professor Goddard's invention the development of rockets was associated with war rather than the exploration of outer space. In the later years of World War II a type of rocket called the V-2, which used alcohol for fuel and liquid oxygen for igniting it and maintaining its ignition, became a major weapon. Launched from the Continent and carrying high explosives, one could accurately hit its target in England.

By the war's end many countries had become interested in rocketry, but the United States and Russia were the two that determined to carry on serious programs in that field. The United States soon set up a proving ground in a desertlike area in New Mexico called White Sands. Its dimensions, 125 miles by 40 miles, seemed to offer plenty of space for the rocket project.

Many experiments were carried out at White Sands, the

most notable being to perfect a "stage" arrangement. The principle was to mount one rocket on top of another—an idea that had been suggested by Professor Goddard years before. Now a V-2 was used for the base and a second rocket was mounted on it. After blast-off the V-2 shot upward twenty miles in less than a minute. Then the second rocket broke free and continued on under its own power until it was almost 250 miles above White Sands. Both rockets dropped back to earth.

Such flights into the upper atmosphere were valuable in bringing back or sending back by electronic impulses, important information on such matters as wind velocity, radiation factors, effects of heat caused by friction, and the molecular composition of those upper regions.

But even as such tests were being carried out, the V-2 rockets were becoming outdated. New designs were being worked on, and of particular interest was the type called Viking. The first Viking of a series, launched in August 1951, sped upward 135 miles at a maximum speed of more than four thousand miles an hour. It carried cameras which were able to photograph the earth from that high altitude.

With growing successes White Sands became too small for the great rocket project, and a new site was selected in Florida. It was named Cape Canaveral (later changed to Cape Kennedy, then renamed Canaveral) and was to become the setting for highly dramatic moments—tragic as well as successful—in space exploration.

Even before White Sands had ceased to function, the Canaveral launching pads were ready for action. The great advantage of Canaveral was that because it was near the coastline, after their ascent, rockets would fall into the ocean and be no danger to inland areas.

The United States space program was progressing, but it was hampered by lack of funds and no exciting breakthroughs were taking place. Then came a development that startled the whole world: On October 4, 1957, the Russians launched a satellite that, some three hundred miles up, went into orbit around the earth.

The satellite, called Sputnik, had been launched by rockets in three stages, being ejected in the third stage while the rocket-conveyor was moving at about eighteen thousand miles an hour. Little Sputnik (it was only about the size of a football) could not be seen with the naked eye as it moved across the heavens but, thanks to its radio transmitter, it could send out signals to be picked up on earth. Sputnik I stayed in orbit for three months, then fell toward earth, being destroyed as it sped through the atmosphere.

Looking back, twenty years later, Sputnik seems an unspectacular achievement, but at that time it was quite miraculous. People wondered if it might disrupt the moon or eventually crash down on their homes. But regardless of any fears, they regarded it as a triumph, a triumph that had not been won by the United States. Blazing headlines proclaimed that the Space Age really had arrived—and that Russia was its leader.

As a result Americans, from the "man on the street" to the country's President, were in a state of shock. It was felt that the educational system of the United States, its scientific advances, and its capabilities in general were no longer first-rate. It was felt also that some extraordinary achievement in outer space must be carried out to restore American pride and prestige.

Nevertheless for the next several years there was still an unwillingness to devote enormous amounts of money to a space program. Research went along quietly, therefore, while Russia launched bigger and better Sputniks, and even carried out probes with a Lunik that crash-landed on the moon and another that took excellent pictures of the moon's far side. Then came another spectacular Russian "first." In April 1961 a man was launched in a spacecraft that went into orbit and circled the earth in approximately one and a half hours. The man, Yuri Gagarin, had become the world's first astronaut.

Now there was real consternation in the United States, and the "something must be done" thinking quickly changed to action. Urgent meetings were called between NASA (created in 1958) and government officials to consider how much money could be assigned to space, and to decide on a goal that would be dramatic, spectacular, and of real importance as the Space Age progressed.

The decision was: Shoot for the moon.

This did not mean merely a crash landing of mechanical devices. It meant for people to land on and explore the moon. Even with a new, almost limitless budget, and with the impressive start toward space travel that already had been made, such exploration could not be achieved overnight. But work toward that goal now went forward with new speed and determination.

The United States already had launched a number of rockets, some carrying small monkeys, and one with a chimpanzee named Ham as a passenger. (Ham became something of a national hero, and since his rocket trip, has been living comfortably at the National Zoo in Washington, D.C.) The next step would be to put a man into space.

On May 5, 1961, Alan Shepard, Jr., was strapped into the cabin of a thirty-three-ton spacecraft called Mercury, which was shot out through the earth's atmosphere by a rocket named Redstone. Shepard's trip took him only about 300 miles, and he went no higher than 115 miles; he did not go into orbit. But when he splashed down in perfect shape in the Atlantic Ocean, the venture was considered a great success. It renewed optimism about reaching the moon.

Three months later there was another suborbital flight. Little more than six months after that, the spacecraft Mercury 6 went into orbit carrying John Glenn, Jr. It circled the earth three times in a flight that lasted almost five hours.

Now the United States was investing billions of dollars in its space program, with the moon as its acknowledged objective. Russia, also, was continuing to probe outer space. Many satellites were put into space by both countries. And astronauts from each country were experimenting with "space walks."

When the time came actually to land on the moon, two astronauts would have to leave a large spaceship, handled by a third companion, and in another craft—the lunar module—would go to the moon's surface. When their exploration was completed, the men would lift off, meet the parent spacecraft, and dock with it.

Space walks contributed important experience for such a maneuver. With mission after mission the project called Gemini was making docking in outer space an exciting new science.

Another project being carried out concerned a type of rocket called Ranger, which would someday take cameras to the moon. The first Ranger launchings were disappointing, but Ranger 7 "paid off." In July 1964 it became the first successful American moon probe as it crashed in

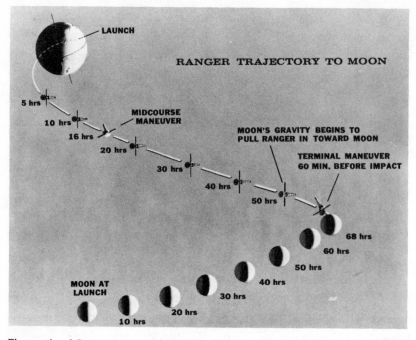

 — the image contains the following labels:

LAUNCH

RANGER TRAJECTORY TO MOON

5 hrs

10 hrs

MIDCOURSE MANEUVER

16 hrs

20 hrs

MOON'S GRAVITY BEGINS TO PULL RANGER IN TOWARD MOON

30 hrs

TERMINAL MANEUVER 60 MIN. BEFORE IMPACT

40 hrs

50 hrs

68 hrs

60 hrs

50 hrs

40 hrs

MOON AT LAUNCH

30 hrs

20 hrs

10 hrs

The path of Ranger—a rocket project designed to take close-up photographs of the moon.

the Sea of Clouds after sending back to earth more than four thousand photos of the moon's surface. Ranger 8 landed on the Sea of Tranquillity, the area which was to become the target for the first landing by astronauts. It, also, transmitted excellent pictures.

While rockets and missiles were going up from the great launching pads at Cape Canaveral, a huge development was growing in Texas—the Manned Spacecraft Center at Houston. It had begun in 1961 with a half-dozen people who used a shopping center as headquarters. By 1966 the staff consisted of thousands of employees. Working in a complex that had cost more than 300 million dollars, they were checking out and testing spacecraft. And from there Mission Control would guide astronauts on their way to the moon.

Along with such gigantic projects as Mercury, Gemini, and Ranger, another one, Project Apollo, was taking shape. The goal was to develop a three-man spaceship that could circle the earth—or the moon—for extended periods. It would be blasted from its launch pad by a mighty rocket, Saturn V.

The second stage of the rocket Saturn V (eighty-one feet long) being transported by an ocean-going barge to a launch complex at Cape Canaveral. It is shown passing through the opened Banana River Bridge. Later, Saturn V would be the rocket to launch Apollo 10.

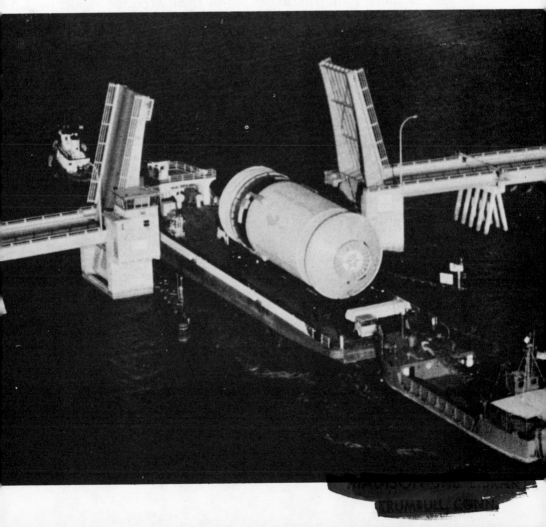

TRUMBULL CONN.

The Apollo program was so complex it becomes difficult for a mind to grasp all the scientific and engineering skills that were involved. Two million working parts were used in the spacecraft alone; something like 300,000 people at one point or another worked on it.

At last Apollo 1 stood ready for its earth-orbital shot, and on January 27, 1967, three astronauts, Virgil Grissom, Edward White, and Roger Chaffee, wearing their space suits, entered the cabin to take part in testing the communications system and take-off procedures as a rehearsal for their flight. But the tests were not to be completed. When the men had been in the spacecraft for more than five hours, talking with controllers on the outside, a sudden interruption came in their expected reporting:

"We've got a fire in the spacecraft."

These words, spoken by Chaffee, were a prelude to stark tragedy. For a combination of reasons, it was impossible for the astronauts to escape, and within eighteen seconds they were dead from asphyxiation. The fire raged until Apollo 1 was nothing but a charred ruin.

Strangely, the first tragedy in the Russian space program occurred only three months later. That country had launched a manned craft which apparently was intended to meet another craft in space and dock with it. However, the plans were not carried out; the end of the mission came with a crash landing in which the pilot, Colonel Vladimir Komarov, was killed.

In the United States hundreds of experts were still going over the charred remains of Apollo 1. Work was progressing on a new spacecraft, with countless suggestions being made concerning changes. But the grief still felt over the loss of Chaffee, White, and Grissom, and the dis-

Providing food for astronauts during a mission was one of the first concerns in planning for long space flights. These packages successfully carried chicken, beef with gravy, cereal, chocolate beverage, fruit juices, and bread substitutes.

Having a drink of orange juice in a Gemini rocket capsule was somewhat different from having it during breakfast at home.

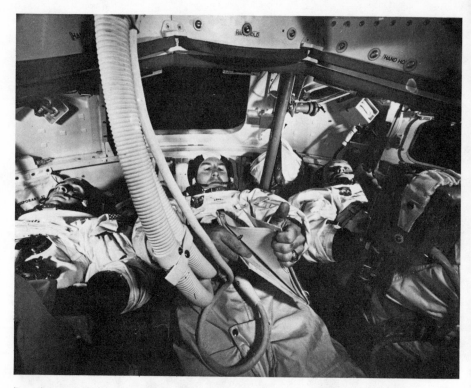

Practicing for the Apollo 8 orbital flight. The crew—William Anders, James Lovell, and Frank Borman—are shown getting ready for this mission which went into orbit around the moon and returned safely to earth.

couragement over the setback to moon travel, created a gloomy atmosphere at Canaveral.

Nevertheless, little more than nine months after the fire, a bigger and better Apollo—Apollo 4—stood on the launch pad ready for an unmanned trial run. Its success was followed by others, including Apollo 8, which carried Frank Borman, James Lovell, and William Anders to lunar orbit and safely back to earth.

By the time Apollo 10 was ready for action, its crew

members—Thomas Stafford, John Young, and Eugene Cernan—were anxious to make an actual moon landing. But this idea was not approved, and they had to be satisfied with making final tests for that historic mission to be carried out on the next flight.

However, these astronauts went closer to the moon than anyone had been before, and they separated the lunar module from the spacecraft and docked it again. During the mission they enjoyed a bit of relaxation with music ("Up, Up, and Away" was their theme song), and they

Apollo missions were concluded with a "splash-down" in the ocean, where the astronauts could be picked up by helicopter and flown to a waiting ship. Here Apollo 9 has landed some hundreds of miles away from Cape Canaveral.

were pleased with the friendly names they had given their spaceship and the lunar module. The spacecraft was Charlie Brown; the lunar module, Snoopy.

It was a joyous moment when, close to the moon, the lunar module was separated and then docked with the spacecraft. The report came through to Mission Control: "Snoopy and Charlie Brown are hugging each other!"

Charlie Brown returned safely to earth, while Snoopy was turned loose to become a satellite of the sun. Meanwhile, back at Cape Canaveral, another spacecraft, Apollo 11, was ready and waiting for action.

Snoopy, shown here with Astronaut Thomas Stafford, became a symbol for the Manned Flight Awareness Program of NASA. His name was given also to the lunar module of Apollo 10, and the spacecraft for that mission was christened Charlie Brown.

5

Men on the Moon:
The Apollo Missions

On July 20, 1969, at 4:17 P.M. Eastern Daylight Saving Time, a voice, quiet but triumphant, spoke to Mission Control at Houston:

"Houston, Tranquillity Base here. The Eagle has landed."

The voice was that of astronaut Neil Armstrong, commander of the Apollo 11 mission to the moon. The Eagle was the lunar module. And this was the historic moment when the hopes of earthbound people to explore this distant satellite were finally realized.

After the 240,000-mile journey from the earth, Armstrong and Edwin Aldrin, Jr., who was pilot of the Eagle, rested for several hours in its cabin. Then, wearing his space suit and supporting a backpack filled with equipment to help him breathe in this world where there was no air, Armstrong pushed open the hatch and slowly climbed down a nine-rung ladder. One more step and he was actually standing on the moon!

A few moments later the astronaut cautiously walked a short distance away from the Eagle; then almost immediately he began to collect samples of soil, using a scoop especially designed for this mission. He worked as fast as possible, storing several pounds of soil and small rocks in a bag, which he then put in a leg pocket of his space suit. In case anything happened that would force an unexpectedly early departure, such as a leak developing in his

"There they go!" Members of the Space Center government-industry team at Cape Canaveral rise from their monitoring consoles to watch the Apollo 11 lift-off. This was the first attempt ever made to land men on the moon. It succeeded.

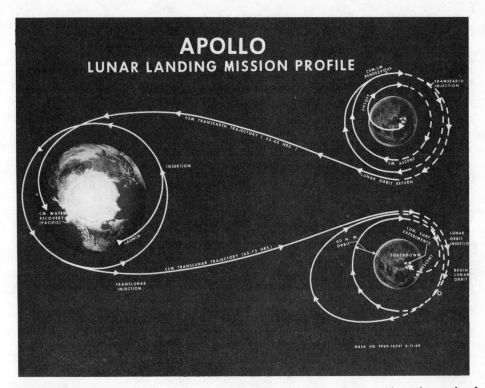

APOLLO
LUNAR LANDING MISSION PROFILE

NASA HQ FP69-16541 6-11-69

Every detail was considered before the Apollo 11 mission began. Here the path of the spaceship is charted from lift-off on earth, through lunar orbit and touch-down, to recovery in the Pacific Ocean.

This photograph of the moon was taken (from a distance of 10,000 miles) by the crew of the Apollo 11 spacecraft as they came back to earth after their historic trip to the moon. On it, their landing site is pointed out, and the expected landing site for the Apollo 17 mission—the Taurus-Littrow valley.

The Eagle has landed! Astronaut Edwin Aldrin leaves footprints in the dust as he moves a short distance from the lunar module soon after it landed on the moon. The picture was taken by his companion, Neil Armstrong, commander of the Apollo 11 mission.

suit, he would not return to earth without some moon samples.

As he worked, he talked into equipment that carried his voice to Houston, describing everything he saw in the moon-world, and he moved a television camera from the lunar module to set it up where it could convey pictures of himself and Aldrin as they worked.

Then it was time to be joined on the moon's dusty surface by Aldrin. The men would have no more than two hours to become adjusted to this strange world. It was not only without air; there was no sound, not even the faint stirring of a breeze. And because gravity was different from that on earth, the weight of everything (including themselves) was different. But in spite of the strangeness, they concentrated on their work, while the third astronaut of the team, Michael Collins, continued in orbit with the command and service modules until it was time for a reunion.

Armstrong and Aldrin each had two cameras. One was suspended at a convenient height in front of the body, the other was mounted near one end of a rod. The rod, carried like a cane, could be pushed down when desired and this would activate a flash that resulted in two pictures being taken. Close-ups of the moon's surface could not be obtained otherwise because, in their bulky space suits, the astronauts had to stand almost completely upright.

Even though they could not bend, they were able to make a good collection of moon samples. Besides the aluminum scoop for gathering soil, they also had tongs with which to pick up stones too big to fit in the scoop and a hammer to break small pieces from boulders. Both these tools could be fitted into an extension handle.

In order to reach samples well beneath the surface, Aldrin pushed, then pounded hollow tubes into the soil. For three inches the tubes moved down easily. After that they met strong resistance, and although Aldrin hammered with all his strength, they would go no farther than nine inches. Strangely, after being imbedded to that depth, they would not stay erect. Because the material into which they were forced was so firm, there was every reason to believe they would stand upright. Here was a mystery to ponder.

Other activities of Armstrong and Aldrin involved work that would continue long after they had returned to earth. One of the activities was setting up four seismometers, which would record the slightest tremor on the moon as well as any great shock caused by the crashing of a meteorite or a "moonquake."

There was also a laser mirror to be set up and adjusted. This would serve later in several ways. When a laser beam (concentrated bands of light) was sent toward it from earth, it would reflect the beam back to a telescope. Scientists could use these communicating signals to learn of the fluctuations in the earth's rate of rotation and in motions of the polar axis. By such means they could also measure continental drift on the earth. A still further use for the laser-mirror beam would be to measure more accurately than before the distance between moon and earth.

A further important apparatus to be set up was one that could test the composition of solar wind. This, unlike wind on the earth, which is actually moving atmosphere, results from explosions on the sun.

When Armstrong and Aldrin climbed back into their LM, carrying airtight containers of moon rocks, two hours of amazing accomplishment had been achieved. The next accomplishment was to rejoin the parent spacecraft and dock with it. Then, after moving into it with their collections, they turned the Eagle adrift in outer space. Rocket engines of the service module were fired—and the Apollo 11 expedition was on its way back to earth.

Technically the mission had been a fantastic success. It proved that a round trip from earth to moon could be achieved. Communication systems had checked out efficiently. Space suits and other apparatus designed to keep earth people alive on the moon had done their job.

But in spite of all that had been accomplished, some

The first space suit worn by men on the moon, the astronauts of Apollo 11. Changes were made for those used on later missions, but the essential life-sustaining features and work-aids were all continued.

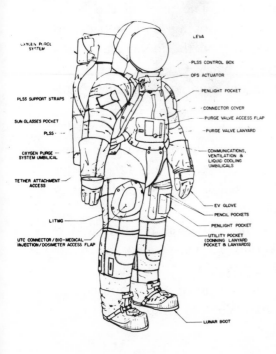

scientists were not entirely happy about the mission. They were anxious for more "samples" of the moon, and they wished that photographs had been taken to show the exact setting in which each collection had been made. On earth when fossils are discovered and taken from their rocky surroundings, photographs and charts of the setting are helpful for later studies of the prehistoric remains. In somewhat the same way the exact positions in which moon rocks were found could have some bearing on their history.

Therefore when plans were being made for the Apollo 12 mission, scientific studies were emphasized. Another project scheduled was the recovery of material from the rocket Surveyor 3, which had landed on the moon in 1966 and was still standing in the Ocean of Storms. So the Ocean of Storms was made the target for Apollo 12.

The skipper of this mission was Charles Conrad, Jr., already an experienced spaceman. The pilot of the lunar module was Alan Bean, who was making his first trip into outer space. He would be walking on the moon and working with fellow astronaut Richard Gordon, Jr., while Conrad continued in orbit in the command module, Yankee Clipper.

Much had been learned from the experiences of Apollo 11 that was put to use in the new mission. And the crew, this time, could actually see their destination—the Ocean of Storms—from the earth. It seemed the second journey to the moon would have clear sailing.

However, this was not to be. Little more than half a minute after launching, Apollo 12 was struck by lightning. Seconds later it was struck again.

A mystery! There had been no sign of a lightning storm anywhere near the launch area. What had happened?

Investigations later revealed the answer: As the huge Apollo vehicle left the earth, it was trailed by its own ionized exhaust which extended downward like a fan. This acted as an electrical conductor between electrical forces in low clouds and the ground. Apollo 12 rose quickly between two layers of the clouds, and, as it did, all their electricity was discharged.

This alarming development did disable instruments temporarily, but by great good fortune no major disaster resulted. Apollo 12 continued its thrust beyond the earth's atmosphere, and eighty-three hours later it was in orbit around the moon. During its third revolution the lunar module, the Intrepid, carrying Conrad and Bean, was cast off from the parent ship. As the LM dropped, Conrad stood at the controls, while Bean monitored the guidance computer and reported velocity changes.

Soon the vehicle had been slowed to a rate of three feet per second, then two. Then contact was made with the moon's surface. Gentle as the landing was, it raised a tremendous cloud of dust, making it impossible to see through the module's windows.

Conrad lost no time checking the supply of fuel in the LM that had been stored to use for lift-off when the time came to rejoin the Yankee Clipper. Such fuel was saved especially for that purpose, so an adequate supply surely would be there—unless some leak had developed. In that dreadful event, the astronauts would be stranded on the moon!

Conrad found the supply intact (there was no problem in this area during any of the Apollo missions), and he and Bean could start thinking ahead to the thirty-one and a half hours they would spend on the moon. This would be ten hours more than the total time that had been available to Armstrong and Aldrin. Another important change in the mission was that Conrad and Bean would be able to walk (or hop) in their space suits as far as half a mile from their LM.

The astronauts had something else to think about with satisfaction and pleasure: Their landing, due to their own skills and expert guidance from Mission Control back in Houston, had been a complete success. Not only had they come down on the Ocean of Storms, they were only six hundred feet from their planned target, Surveyor 3.

Impatient to start their explorations, Conrad and Bean helped each other into their space suits, then made their way down the ladder. In the four hours that followed they worked constantly, setting up equipment and collecting rocks and soil samples, talking with Houston as they did so. The space suits still made activity awkward, but they were perfect for survival. A liquid cooling system and an oxygen-purge system were two of the devices in each.

Back in their LM, though claiming they were not tired, the explorers managed to sleep for five hours, having the luxury of hammocks in which to rest. In Apollo 11, the floor had been the only resting place.

The big challenge of making contact with the rocket, Surveyor 3, still lay ahead. For two years and five months it had been standing at the rim of a crater—a situation which caused some concern at Mission Control because, to reach it, Conrad and Bean would have to walk through the crater. Would the astronauts sink into deep dust as they made this journey?

For years dust had been a dreaded factor in all thinking about possible moon travel, and some worry about it still lingered. At certain places, could it be deep enough for a person to "drown"? A crater would be a likely place for it to accumulate to this extent.

But all went well. Conrad and Bean moved cautiously, and soon they were able to report to Houston that, underneath its dust covering, the ground was firm. As they came close to Surveyor 3, they found that its coating, originally white, had changed to a light tan. However, they quickly discovered this was not actual discoloring; the entire vehicle was coated with fine dust. It seemed strange that this was tan, because the dust that covered the ground was gray.

Following plans that had been outlined before they left the earth, they took the television camera from the Surveyor rocket, a portion of the camera's cable which they cut off, and some aluminum tubing and glass. With all this packed into an equipment bag, they made their way back to the Intrepid.

With further collections made and other assignments carried out, Conrad and Bean checked and rechecked with control at Houston until all systems were "go" for a lift-off from the Ocean of Storms. In about three hours they had made connections with the Yankee Clipper—and it was time to say goodbye to the Intrepid, which had served them so well.

This time the lunar module was not cast into outer space. It was released so that it would fall back to the moon. When it hit the surface, about forty miles from the site to which it had taken Conrad and Bean, the seismometers that had been left on the moon by the Apollo 11 mission started to reverberate. It was rather a deafening proof that these recording instruments were in good working order.

Two expeditions having been carried out with great

technical success, Mission Control and the crew for Apollo 13 were especially enthusiastic about their moon venture. James Lovell was crew commander; Fred Haise, Jr., was his partner for the lunar module; John Swigert, Jr., was the pilot for the spacecraft, christened the Odyssey. The landing site chosen was the Fra Mauro area, about 110 miles east of the area where Apollo 12 had landed.

The blast-off from Canaveral was, as usual, spectacular and, as the Odyssey shot moonward, it appeared to be on its way to another successful expedition. But all was not well. Nearly fifty-six hours later, Swigert, speaking to Houston, suddenly interrupted a conversation about photographing a comet with the startling information, "Hey, we've got a problem here."

There was indeed a problem. A tank of liquid oxygen had exploded in the service module, blowing out the module's side. The spaceship began to pitch and roll.

Anxiously the crew discussed the problem with ground control, and it was decided that their only hope lay in all three squeezing into the lunar module, then later changing into the command module, which, if all went well, could bring them back to earth. It would be impossible to return in the LM because that module had no heat shield and therefore could not survive speeding through the earth's atmosphere.

With great calm Lovell, Haise, and Swigert continued to talk with ground control and carry out necessary assignments. When the right time came, they separated the damaged service module from the command module, letting it drift away into space. Then, after more than sixty hours in the LM, word came to crawl into the command module and power its storage batteries. Soon afterward the Odyssey was headed for a splash-down in the Pacific Ocean, where the astronauts were picked up by a helicopter and flown to the deck of an aircraft carrier which had been standing by.

These breath-taking events were watched by millions of people on television, and there were worldwide feelings of thankfulness and amazement at the happy ending. However, as soon as the suspense was over, a general wave of criticism against the Apollo program was begun. "So much money being spent on needless moon exploring! It should be used for much-needed programs on earth." This became an outcry and, as a result, there were serious cutbacks in the Apollo budgets for future work.

Nevertheless activities were continuing. Investigations revealed the cause of the damage to Apollo 13, and plans were made for another moon landing, with improvements made to the spacecraft equipment. By January 1971 Apollo 14 was launched.

Once again the target was to be Fra Mauro, but a different crew was aboard this time. The astronauts were Edgar Mitchell, Alan Shepard, Jr., and Stuart Roosa, with Roosa the pilot of the command module, Kitty Hawk.

A couple of problems did arise during the flight, but both were solved, and several days after blast-off the LM, called Antares, touched down on the moon almost exactly on target. Shepard and Mitchell lost no time getting to work amid the rough terrain of Fra Mauro, setting up scientific equipment and a television camera.

The chief objective of their studies was to be Cone Crater, and because of the exactness of their landing, it was not a far walk. This was fortunate. It was an uphill climb and the moon-walkers had a two-wheeled cart to pull, in which they carried a variety of work equipment and into which they put the samples they were collecting.

Before long Mitchell and Shepard found their hearts were beating faster than normal, and they had some difficulty in breathing. But undaunted, and thrilled by the strangely beautiful setting they were in, they continued on to Cone Crater. When they finally returned to Antares, they turned on the television set so that their departure from the moon could be seen on earth.

But before they left, Shepard put on a surprise act. He showed that he held a golf ball in his left hand. Then he dropped it and, using an improvised golf club, swung at it —and missed. This was not to be wondered at, because, with his stiff space suit, he could use only one arm. However, the two additional swings he made both sent the ball flying.

After that "first golf game on the moon," it was a climb back into Antares for Shepard and Mitchell, and soon they were docking with the Kitty Hawk. On the way back to earth they continued work, carrying on experiments regarding gravity that would be useful in future space programs.

After their return Roosa, Shepard, and Mitchell provided an important milestone in our knowledge of the moon. Since the beginning of the missions, returning astronauts had been held in quarantine for lengthy periods to make sure that no micro-organisms had come back to earth with them. None had been discovered. Now after this crew had been quarantined, and no sign of any organism could be found, and as no evidence of fossil organisms showed up in their rock samples, scientists came to a conclusion: No form of life exists, or ever did exist, on the moon.

Six months later NASA was ready for the next mission. The spacecraft for Apollo 15, named Endeavor, had a crew consisting of David Scott, James Irwin, and Alfred Worden, and they had something new to take to the moon: a "moon buggy," more properly called a lunar rover or LR.

The LR had four wheels, was powered by batteries, and was capable of riding over the moon's rough surface at speeds up to eight miles an hour. In it Scott and Irwin could drive several miles on their rock hunts; earlier astronauts had been limited to much shorter distances.

While Worden stayed in orbit, Scott and Irwin brought the lunar module, Falcon, down to the slope of a crater. They were at Hadley Rille, the base from which they would explore rilles, craters, and plains. But first they had to unload the LR from its storage space in the Falcon. This proved to be a more difficult job than it had seemed in practice sessions on earth, but finally it was released and ready for action.

Among other improvements that had been developed in time for this mission was a new type of space suit. It was more flexible in the neck and waist, and the wearer could turn, twist, and bend more easily.

For three days the astronauts traveled, collected, and made countless photographs. They saw Mount Hadley rising almost fifteen thousand feet above the plain, and the Apennine Mountains, which dwarfed everything around them. Among the rocks they found were some beautiful crystals—especially exciting because they could be evidence of early volcanic action on the moon.

The explorers drilled into the moon so they could measure the heat under its surface, hoping to check to a depth of ten feet. They could not quite reach that goal

Something new for the moon explorers of Apollo 15 was a lunar rover, or "moon buggy," which is shown at the right on this photograph. It was packed into a bay of the lunar module with wheels folded against the chassis. Pulling it out and opening it after landing proved a tough job. The LM is at the center of the picture. To the left, James Irwin salutes the flag.

The lunar rover is shown at the edge of Hadley Rille. Its weight on earth
was 460 pounds, but on the moon a mere 76 pounds, so that it could
be lifted by one man.

In this view of the moon, as seen from the Apollo 16 spacecraft, the astronauts looked across the Sea of Crises into the Sea of Tranquillity— a portion of which shows here at the upper right. The bright-rayed crater (slightly to the right of center) is Proclus.

but, with the use of a core tube, they extracted samples from nearly seven feet down.

After three excursions in the LR, it was time for Scott and Irwin to rejoin the Endeavor. They had roamed the moon's surface for 18½ hours, which was about double the time spent outside the LM by Apollo 14 astronauts. They had introduced a power-driven, wheeled vehicle to the moon. They had gathered 173 pounds of rocks.

Apollo 15 had been eventful and rewarding. But now only two more missions would be carried out. Due to cutbacks in the Apollo budget, several originally planned had been canceled.

Apollo 16 was to aim for a furrowed, hilly area called Descartes, near the center of the moon. The scientific studies to be carried out seemed almost overwhelming, for it was hoped that information gathered would be more extensive than from all four previous missions put together. Scientists were most anxious for facts that would shed light on how mountains of the moon had been formed in contrast to the earth's mountains. Altogether this mission had weighty responsibilities.

The crew involved in all these accomplishments included John Young, Charles Duke, Jr., and Thomas Mattingly. The spaceship was named Casper; the lunar module, Orion.

Blast-off in April 1972 went perfectly, but when Orion was separated from Casper, a serious situation was discovered: There was a bad circuit in the backup steering system that controlled Orion's main rocket engine. After Orion was on the moon, if its prime system failed for any reason, and the backup was not functioning, the astronauts would have no way of returning to earth.

Casper, piloted by Mattingly, continued orbiting the moon while the problem was discussed with flight directors at Houston. Finally (after fifteen revolutions around the moon) the decision was made to carry out a landing in spite of the bad circuit. After all, the prime system was in perfect condition. Orion, it was felt, could "make the grade."

Young and Duke agreed wholeheartedly with the decision, and soon Orion was on its way to Descartes. Making up for the extra time spent in orbit, the two men hurried into action, pulling their lunar rover from its storage place and setting up all kinds of equipment including an ultraviolet camera-spectrograph.

The drill on this mission was much improved over that used by Apollo 15, and it did not take long to bore a ten-foot hole. Then a fiberglass rod easily went down into it. Now more evidence could be gathered about the moon's internal heat.

The first trip away from Orion in the LR lasted more than seven hours but, although extremely tired, the astronauts were eagerly looking forward to more exploring, more collecting. Before leaving on this mission, both had spent many hours studying rocks with geologists from universities, the U. S. Geological Survey, and NASA's spacecraft center. They fully appreciated the significance of the rocks they were able to collect from the highlands of the moon.

When Young and Duke entered Orion for the last time, ready for lift-off, there was one unusual problem to deal with. Orange juice had leaked from one of the containers held in the neckband of a space suit, and turned into a gluelike substance. It was a tussle to take off a helmet in that sticky situation.

However, Young and Duke were ready to follow the "Go" command when it came from Houston. They shot up from the moon, and soon all three astronauts were together again in Casper, heading for home.

Thousands of people gathered at the Canaveral Space Center to watch the blast-off of Apollo 17. It was especially dramatic because it took place at night, and the fiery explosion from the rocket could be seen many hundreds of miles away. It was dramatic also because this was the final Apollo mission—the conclusion of a program that had worked miracles in probing outer space and putting men on the moon.

The command module for Apollo 17 was christened America; the lunar module, Challenger. The moon target chosen was a wide valley bordered by three mountains which, at some points, rose thousands of feet from their base. This mountainous area, named Taurus, was situated near a giant crater called Littrow; between lay the Taurus-Littrow valley.

Eugene Cernan, who had already logged hundreds of hours in space, and held degrees in electrical engineering and aeronautical engineering, was commander of the mission. Ronald Evans would be the one to stay in orbit, waiting for Cernan and Jack Schmitt to carry on their explorations.

Schmitt had a unique background for his assignments. Although he had trained at the Air Force Flight School, he was, first of all, a geologist. As a boy he had gone rock-hunting in southwestern deserts and Indian reservations. Later, with a doctorate in geology, he joined the U. S. Geological Survey at Flagstaff, Arizona, and as soon as NASA began recruiting scientist-astronauts, he applied. With Apollo 17 he would be a copilot, and also the first true earth scientist to reach the moon.

Just after midnight, between December 6 and 7, 1972, the America took off from its launch pad. On December 11 the Challenger was set down in the Taurus-Littrow valley, only three hundred feet off its exact target.

When Schmitt and Cernan hurried out to the moon's surface, Schmitt's opinion, carried back to earth, was, "a geologist's paradise if ever I saw one." However, as a geologist with endless experience collecting earth rocks, he soon admitted to unexpected difficulties in picking up moon rocks while wearing a bulky space suit and becoming accustomed to the moon's weak gravity.

Cernan, in his enthusiasm, swung a geological hammer at a boulder so hard it ended up knocking part of a rear fender off the lunar rover.

The rear fenders had a very special purpose. They were to shield the astronauts, and the vehicle, from the heavy spray of moon dust that flew up as the wheels turned. With no "auto-body repair shop" at hand, Cernan and Schmitt tried to mend the fender with tape, but this attempt was not successful because the fine-grained lunar dust prevented it from sticking.

Soon Mission Control at Houston asked them to leave the LR and begin setting up lunar surface experiments. However, when it was time for the next expedition in the LR, Mission Control had an excellent suggestion: Tape together four lunar maps made of stiff photographic paper, which would form a heavy 15-by-19-inch sheet. This could be attached to the fender with clamps taken from the lunar module's light fixtures.

The idea worked perfectly. Dust was directed backward and kept under control even when the "buggy" was racing along at seven miles an hour!

Exploring, collecting, and photographing continued successfully for two more days. Great excitement was created by the discovery of an area of orange soil—extraordinary because it could mean there had been volcanic activity in fairly recent times.

After a third expedition in the LR, it was time for Cernan and Schmitt to leave the moon. The emergency paper fender had served its purpose well. The astronauts had been able to collect 250 pounds of rocks, and many clumps of soil (including the mysterious orange-colored); they had taken thousands of photographs, and had reams of scientific data.

Explorations by Project Apollo were now at an end, but this did not mean an end to studies resulting from it. Rocks and soil samples were distributed among scientists of many countries to be analyzed, and a watch was continued on instruments such as seismometers that were still operating on the moon.

Much had been learned. Proven facts had replaced fantasy and guesswork. And any age-old thoughts that people might someday enjoy living on the moon had been dismissed. Now citizens of the earth began to accept the moon as a neighboring planet instead of looking at it as a distant circle of a silver-colored substance about which myths and folklore could be woven. And many scientists felt there was a strong possibility that this small planet would someday help them find logical explanations as to how the universe was created.

6

Dry Seas and Dusty Oceans

To the ancients, astronomer and casual observer alike, the
moon appeared as a bright, though mottled, ball in the
night sky. And it is easy to understand how, to anyone
with imagination, the areas of light and dark could have
resembled such familiar things as a man's face or a rabbit. Galileo's perspicillum (actually a "seeing tube"),
however, brought the lunar surface away from fantasy
and into the world of facts because, even with his very
crude telescope, Galileo was able to identify what appeared to be craters, mountains, and seas. He was accu-
rate about the craters and mountains, but in the "seas" he
was misled.

Just as explorers on earth enjoy naming their discoveries, Galileo and the astronomers who followed him
sought to give names to the outstanding features of the
moon. In doing so they carried on his mistaken impression
of the large, dark, relatively smooth areas on the lunar
surface. He had identified these as seas, bays, and

marshes, giving them the name *maria* (singular: *mare*), which is Latin for "seas."

Even after scientists had proved that the existence of any water on the moon was highly unlikely, the term *maria* continued to be used. The result was very wet names for very dry places.

There are over twenty of these "seas" on the moon, including the famous Sea of Tranquillity, site of the first Apollo landing. The Ocean of Storms, site of the Apollo 12 landing, is a larger sealike area. There are also similar smaller areas, such as the "Marsh of Mists," "Bay of Rainbows," and "Lake of Dreams."

Galileo would have been nearer the truth if he had named these areas deserts, for they are dry and lifeless places, no matter how inviting their lush names make them sound. When viewed closely, they prove not flat, smooth areas; actually, they are wrinkled, rock-littered, crater-pocked plains.

While scientists had long suspected the maria to be the result of great flows of lava, it was not until mare rock samples were brought back by early Apollo missions that actual proof was obtained. The rock was identified as gabbro, a volcanic igneous rock. Further analysis showed samples collected at different sites to be of slightly different composition. This would seem to be the result of individual lava flows. At the Hadley Rille, the Apollo 15 astronauts noticed layering, again pointing to individual flows. It would seem, therefore, that the maria were created by huge outpourings of lava from different parts of the moon some three to four billion years ago. But if volcanism was responsible for the creation of the maria, could it also be the cause of most of the other lunar features?

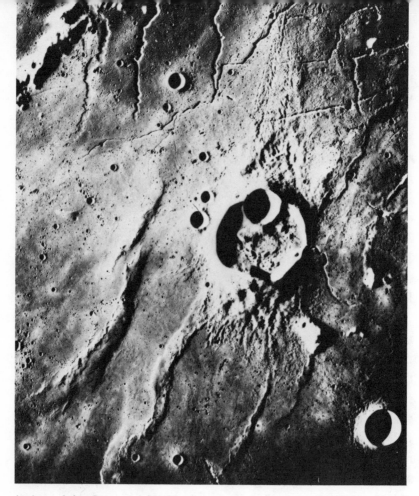

A view of the Ocean of Storms photographed from the Apollo 15 space-craft. Mounds, craters, and rilles are all part of the "Ocean," but not a drop of water exists there.

Scientists have been sharply divided in their opinions. One school felt that internal activity such as volcanism and moonquakes shaped the surface of the moon. To back up this theory they found volcanic craters on earth that closely resemble lunar ones. They also pointed out that other lunar formations such as the Straight Wall in the Sea of Clouds is the result of a "fault"—a slippage of rock along a break in the lunar crust.

Other scientists believed that external forces were responsible for the moon's appearance. For example, they attribute the craters on the moon to meteorite impact.

To confuse the issue even further, a common feature in the lava-created seas are "ghost" craters. These are craters formed on the moon's surface before the lava flowed over them. In some cases the craters are only partially

The maria, or seas, of the moon are dry as dust—and, in fact, they are dust, combined with rocks and boulders. Footprints made there by the astronauts will remain unchanged for there is no moving air to blow the dust away.

The theory that moon craters have been caused by meteors is illustrated here by NASA Research Scientist Donald Gault, as he pictures an impact, sending a spray of moon material out into space. Craters are rare on the earth but are almost everywhere on the moon.

covered, and in others the form of these buried craters is eerily visible beneath the blanket of lava.

Was the moon battered and scarred by the impact of meteors early in its history, or is its pitted surface the result of violent outpourings of molten rock? The answer, according to scientists familiar with the latest Apollo data, lies somewhere in the middle.

The lava flows that formed the maria are definitely volcanic in origin. But the basins that were filled with lava were the sites of meteor bombardment. Following the basin-forming impact, volcanic activity flooded the area with lava.

While meteor impact is seemingly the primary source of lunar craters, there are a number of large, nonimpact craters which must have had volcanic origins. Some of these are the crater chains which indicate fault lines below the lunar surface.

In all there are over a million craters and craterlike formations on the moon. The study of their individual origins will be a problem for scientists to ponder for years to come. We can, however, divide these circular formations into categories according to their physical characteristics.

Walled plains make up the largest of the moon's craters. They are only slightly smaller than some of the seas. Large mountains surround the plains, and both mountains and plains are often pocked with smaller, newer craters.

Ringed plains and craters make up the bulk of the circular formations on the moon's surface and appear to be newer features than the walled plains. Mountains, often as high as several thousand feet, can be found rising from the floor of many of these structures. Some craters, such as Copernicus and Tycho, are called ray craters. Extending outward for hundreds and even, in the case of Tycho, over a thousand miles, are streaks of light, finely pulverized rock called rays. Rays do not extend evenly in all directions. They apparently are particles that have been ejected by their parent crater.

Scientists are not sure why rays are not found with all craters, but they do associate them with the newer craters. Either the lunar surface has changed since the formation of the nonray craters, or erosion has erased all traces of previous rays.

Smaller lunar features include craterlets, domes, crater cones, and crater pits. Craterlets are very small craters ranging from fifty yards to five miles in diameter. They can be found on all parts of the moon, suggesting that they were formed after the other features of the lunar landscape.

Domes and crater cones are far less numerous than craterlets. Although their origins are uncertain, they are probably related to lunar volcanism. Domes are gently sloping rises on the lunar surface. Crater cones resemble volcanoes on earth—small hills with a central depression.

Crater pits are unlike any of the previously mentioned lunar formations. They are small but irregularly shaped depressions, lacking the raised rim of the other lunar craters.

Rilles are long, canyonlike depressions in the surface of the moon. There are two different types which probably have very different origins. Linear rilles are most likely the result of parallel faulting. Sinuous rilles (of which the Hadley Rille, site of Apollo 15's explorations, is an example) are more irregular in their paths. The most likely explanation of their origin is that they are large flow channels produced when lava cut paths through the loosely packed lunar soil known as the regolith. Seen from above, they resemble riverbanks on earth. Other sinuous rilles are believed to be collapsed lava tubes, underground passageways through which lava flowed and exited.

Even though similarities can be seen between many lunar and earthly features, it is the mountains of the moon that bear the greatest resemblance to their earthly counterparts.

Early astronomers, seeing them through a telescope for the first time, were struck by this resemblance and named several of them, such as the Alps, Caucasus, and Pyrenees, after mountain chains on earth.

Before pictures sent back by Ranger 7 and firsthand observations by the Apollo astronauts proved otherwise, mountains on the moon were believed to be rough and jagged. Scientists theorized that on the airless, weatherless moon, mountains would stay preserved for eternity, unchanged from the time of their creation. Surprisingly though, there was very definite evidence of erosion. But this erosion was unlike any earthly form of the process. Over millions of years, impacts by space dust and bombardment by nuclear particles from the solar wind had smoothed the lunar landscape.

One important question remained however: What process caused the creation of these familiar yet strange formations? On earth, mountains are formed in a variety of ways. Faulting, folding, volcanic activity, or a combination of all three can result in the creation of a mountain range. Had it been the same on the moon? Once again, firsthand observations of the Apollo missions provided answers.

Some were most definitely volcanic. Others, such as the Apennines, were created by impact—probably pushed up when a large meteor struck the moon some four billion years ago.

One of the most important discoveries the Apollo missions hoped to make was whether the moon was a "living" or "dead" planet. Living would mean a planet where internal activity had not ceased—on whose surface mountains were still forming and where volcanoes were capable of erupting. This describes a planet like our earth. A dead planet is one which has lost the ability to change, except through external influence such as meteor impact.

When the artist Howard Russell Butler created this painting a number of years ago (long before the Apollo missions) the mountains of the moon were thought to be sharp and jagged. His picture portraying the earth as it would be seen from the moon shows this, with the bit of "moonscape" in the foreground.

During the Apollo 17 mission Astronauts Cernan and Schmitt spent seventy-five hours in the Taurus-Littrow mountainous regions of the moon. Here their lunar rover is parked by a very large boulder with a noticeably "smooth" mountain in the background.

Which kind of planet would the moon prove to be? To explore this question, the Apollo astronauts set up seismometers—instruments to measure tremors or quakes. Two facts appeared as the result of the seismic analysis. Seismically, the moon was a very dead place. Volcanic activity or shifting of the lunar surface was very rare indeed. However, a type of "moonquake" did occur whenever the earth and moon were at perigee—the point when the earth and moon are closest to each other. It is possible to theorize, therefore, that even though the moon has had a very active past, it is now "dead," with only minor changes taking place on its surface.

The Apollo 16 mission carried a special mapping camera to the moon and this is one of the many photographs it took. The area in the upper right is where several missions had left seismometers, and most of the moonquake activity that had been detected over the period of a year came from there.

7

Revelations in the Rocks

As the world awaited the return of the Apollo 11 astronauts, a group of twenty-six scientists were eagerly anticipating the arrival of its precious cargo. Most of them were geologists who would examine the rocks and fine soil which would be returned by the crew to the Lunar Receiving Laboratory in Houston. These samples would initially be handled through "glove boxes" to avoid any possible contamination. A glove box is a sealed compartment in which long-sleeved rubber or plastic gloves are attached to one clear wall. By putting hands in the gloves, a scientist can examine the sample without breaking the seal, thereby exposing the sample to the atmosphere.

It would be important to make such examinations as soon as possible after the rocks left their lunar environment. When the rocks arrived on earth they would be subjected to conditions very different from those on the moon, where they had been lying for millions of years. They were not only bumped and jostled about, they were brought into a more powerful gravitational field and exposed to a far stronger magnetic field than that of the moon. The longer examination was delayed, the greater the danger of losing valuable information. And the more possibilities there would be for earth-caused contamination.

As soon as the rocks and soil had been turned over to them, the scientists began examining, weighing, and photographing. Exercising great care, they chipped off pieces for further chemical, physical, and biological testing. The rocks were then exposed to gases which would help deter-

After the first landing on the moon, Edwin Aldrin lost no time before starting to collect samples of lunar soil and rock as he is shown doing here. In the background the apparatus for solar-wind experiments may be seen.

mine their mineral content and reveal whether they contained any carbon, an ingredient essential for life. When these preliminary examinations had been completed, a report was made, but it was by no means a final one.

Soon more than a hundred teams of scientists had arrived in Houston from different parts of the United States. Each received a few grains of the precious lunar soil or bits of moon rock to take back for laboratory studies.

The lunar rocks were divided into four groups. Type A rocks are igneous—formed by the action of heat. They are fine-grained and dark in color, pocked by little depressions or cavities. Type A rocks appear very similar to the basalts found on earth.

Type B rocks are also igneous. However, while dark in color, they are medium-grained and have larger cavities than Type A. An interesting feature of these rocks is that the depressions often appear to be lined with a glassy material. The rocks bear a resemblance to dolerite, an igneous rock common to earth.

Type C was a breccia, which is a rock formed by particles of different rock, minerals, and glass cemented together by heat and pressure.

Type D consisted of fines—soil particles less than a centimeter in diameter. In this group were minute glass spheres and crystals found in the lunar soil. This soil bears no resemblance to the soil we know on earth as it lacks organic material. Geologists have given it the name regolith (*rego* meaning blanket and *lith* meaning rock).

To the scientists, one of the most interesting features of these Apollo 11 samples was the high concentration of titanium, zirconium, and yttrium—elements found on earth although to a far lesser extent. Whether this proportion of elements was true over the whole moon or merely

A rock sample—basalt gabbro—brought back by the Apollo 15 mission is being tested for its reaction to nitrogen gas.

An electron-microscope photograph of iron crystals which grow in small depressions of lunar breccia.

in the area from which the samples had been gathered was, of course, not known.

The task for the next Apollo mission was clear: Samples would have to be gathered and documented with more accuracy than the Apollo 11 astronauts had had time to do.

In December 1969, a month after Apollo 12 had returned to earth, the Lunar Sample Analysis team was ready with a report. The rocks from the Ocean of Storms, site of Apollo 12's landing, proved younger than those collected by Apollo 11 astronauts from the Sea of Tranquillity by perhaps a billion years.

The system used to calculate the age of the lunar samples is called radiometric dating. It is based on the princi-

At the Manned Spacecraft Center in Houston crew members of the Apollo 14 mission look with keen interest at some of the rocks they have just brought back to earth. Newsmen are in the background.

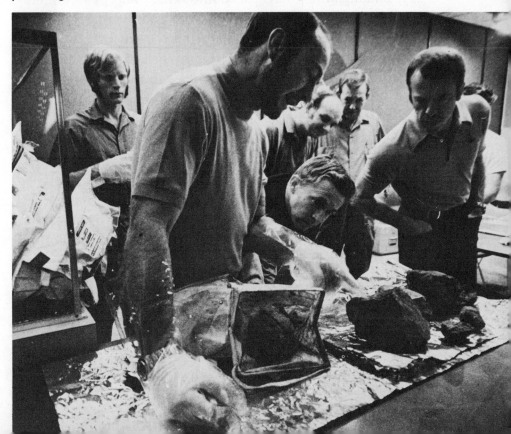

ple that as time passes radioactive elements decay or break down to lighter elements. For example, the most common form of uranium has a half-life of 4.5 billion years. About half of it decays to lead in that time. In other words, if the ratio of uranium to lead is fifty-fifty in a rock, we can assume the rock was formed 4.5 billion years ago.

In the early life of both moon and earth, rocks cooled, hardened, melted, and crystallized over and over again and each cycle reset the atomic clock. Therefore, rocks can be dated only from their last cooling period.

The chemical composition of the rocks from both the Ocean of Storms and the Sea of Tranquillity appeared to be basically the same. The most common mineral found in lunar rock was pyroxene, a calcium-magnesium iron silicate. Other minerals included ilmenite, olivine, and plagioclase. Three new minerals not known on earth were identified in the igneous rock, and were given the names pyroxmanganite, ferropseudobrookite, and chromiumtitanium spinel. Free metallic iron and troilite, both of which are extremely rare on earth, proved to be common accessory minerals in the lunar igneous rock.

It seems that both types of igneous rocks, fine-grained and coarse, are volcanic in nature. They must have been completely molten (liquid) at one time. The faster a rock cools, the smaller its crystals. Since many of the crystals in the lunar basalts are small, it must be assumed that they cooled very near the surface of the moon, or perhaps at its surface.

The samples of lunar basalt with larger crystals that took longer to cool may have been formed in the bottom part of a lava flow, or perhaps from molten rock that never broke through the surface.

Results from the Hadley-Apennine area, site of the Apollo 15 landing, proved that the highlands are different in chemical composition from the low-lying maria. As you can see by looking at the moon, the highlands stand out brightly. This is the result of their aluminum-silicon composition, which reflects more light than the dark, iron-rich maria.

Apollo 17 could claim two major discoveries. One was the startling appearance of orange soil in the Taurus-Littrow region. Its color proved to be the result of glass spheres, some black and others ranging from deep red to light brown. Presumably these were the result of lava flows. This soil may well provide evidence of relatively recent volcanic activity on the moon. The second was the discovery of the oldest rock yet found on the moon. It has been named the Genesis rock.

The Genesis rock proved to be a dunite fragment collected from a blue-gray breccia boulder. The California Institute of Technology dated a chip of this dunite rock at 4.6 billion years. Much of the fragment had managed to survive the pressures and heat that recrystallized the boulder into breccia.

In all, the Apollo missions brought back about 840 pounds of rock and soil. Even though these samples represent a great variety of types, nearly all of the specimens can be put in one of three categories.

There are the mare basalts that make up the dark, relatively smooth maria. "KREEP" norite, a second type, is named for its unusually high content of potassium (K), rare earth elements (REE), and phosphorus (P). The third group, the anorthositic, consists of the most abundant type of lunar rocks. The last two groups make up the moon's highlands.

8

When the Moon Disappears:
Phases and Eclipses

According to the famous poem in *Through the Looking Glass and What Alice Found There,* the Walrus and the Carpenter were walking along a beach while the sun was shining brightly on the sea—a strange state of affairs because it was "the middle of the night." And, the poem continues:

> "The moon was shining sulkily
> Because she thought the sun
> Had no business to be there
> After the day was done."

Nonsensical images are to be expected in Alice's adventures; in real life we do not look for such strange happenings. Yet, as a matter of fact, if we pay close attention to the sky night after night, week after week, we see a number of things that may seem confusing. The moon is continually changing shape from our viewpoint; then it dis-

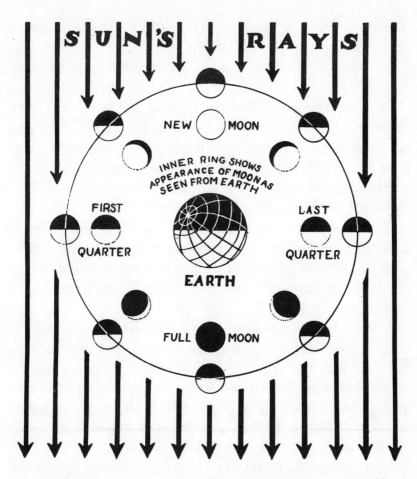

People on earth see the moon in differing phases during its monthly orbit, depending on how much of it is illuminated. The amount visible results from its position in relation to the sun and earth.

appears but returns a few nights later. And although astronomers tell us it travels around the world from west to east, we see it rise in the east and move westward. In the spring we might notice there is a difference of more than an hour between moonrise on one night and the next. But in the autumn the difference between one evening's moonrise and the next may be little more than twenty minutes.

Of course, there are explanations for all these "strange happenings."

Because the moon has no light of its own, it is seen from the earth only as it reflects light from the sun, and an observer on the earth never sees more than half its surface at any one time. As it moves in its orbit around the earth, less and less of the lighted surface is visible. The apparent changes in shape we know as phases.

The impression of an east-to-west journey by the moon is due to the earth's rapid rotation. It is rotating, or spinning, from west to east at such a great speed that, to an observer on earth, the moon is going in the opposite direction.

Variations in the moon's schedule (so much greater than the variations in sunrise schedules) can be traced to the fact that the moon moves at different speeds during its monthly trip around the earth. Its path, or orbit, is not round but elliptical; and when close to the earth, it moves faster than when farther away. These changes in speed are due to the gravitational pull of the earth.

The various lunar phases all have their own names. A lunar month begins with a "new moon." But to our eyes, a *new* moon is no moon at all, because at that time its lighted side is turned away from the earth. For this reason some people call it the "dark of the moon" phase. However, others consider that because it is the period during which a new moon is being created, it is truly "new moon." Calendars that note lunar phases use this name for it rather than "dark of the moon."

When the moon has moved along for one or two evenings, becoming boat shaped as we see only a small slice of it, it is called a "crescent." When it has covered a fourth of its orbit and we see just half of its lighted portion, we call it a "quarter moon." This is a bit confusing, because at that stage it shows as a half moon.

In another week, when the moon is halfway in its orbit and is on one side of the earth while the sun is on the other, we are able to see its entire lighted side, and we call it a "full moon."

From then on, it appears to decrease in size until, in three weeks from its beginning phase, it is again a quarter moon—but this time it is in its last-quarter phase. Then night after night it becomes smaller until it disappears once more.

Other names are used in keeping track of the moon's changing phases: From "new" until it becomes "full" it is called a "waxing" (or growing) moon. From "full" back to "new" it is a "waning" moon. When rounder than half moon but less round than full, it is a "gibbous" moon. These various stages are the result of the moon's revolutions around the earth.

As the moon revolves about the earth, it is spinning slowly on its axis, and its period of rotation is exactly equal to its period of revolution—each taking about twenty-eight days. The speed of rotation at its equator is little more than ten miles per hour. By contrast, the earth at its equator spins at a rate of about a thousand miles an hour.

Because of the equal timing of the moon's rotations and revolutions, its same side is always facing the earth.

Before expeditions could be sent to the moon—even before satellites could be sent into outer space—the natural laws of gravity, motion, and acceleration had to be understood. These laws, first discovered nearly three hundred

An artist's interpretation of how the earth could look from the moon. The earth would appear to change shape in a manner similar to the phases of the moon and here a ''crescent earth'' is visualized.

A photographic plate was exposed at regular intervals during a lunar eclipse; the result shows the gradual progress of the eclipse as the earth moved between the sun and moon.

years ago by the English scientist Sir Isaac Newton, helped astronomers find reasons for the movements of planets and their satellites.

Newton proved that a body in motion remains in motion and tends to travel in a straight line *unless* it is acted upon by some other force. This is known as the law of inertia. In the case of the moon, that other force is the gravitational pull of the earth. This balances the force of inertia which, if unchecked, would cause the moon to go sailing off into space. The moon's orbit is the result of a balance between the force of gravity and the force of inertia.

Besides its disappearance in the course of its monthly revolutions around the earth, the moon vanishes on other occasions. This happens during a lunar eclipse, and it happens simply because the earth has moved between the sun and moon. Then the earth, with the sun shining on it from one side, casts a great, tapering shadow on the other. In length, the shadow is about 860,000 miles.

There are two parts to this giant shadow. There is an elongated dark inner core—the umbra—and this is bordered by wider shadows of lighter gray—the penumbra. As the moon moves slowly into and through the penumbra, we do not see much change in its brightness. But when it enters the dark umbra, it disappears except for a dull coppery glow.

This "mysterious" glow is caused by the earth's atmosphere blending with the long red wavelengths of sunlight. A similar glow may also be seen during crescent phases. When the moon is low in the western sky, appearing as a bright crescent, the rest of its disk may show up in the reddish light reflected from the earth. The glow is commonly called earthshine.

In a lunar eclipse the moon may stay in the umbra for as long as an hour and a half. Then it moves out to the penumbra and perhaps an hour may elapse before it passes through this lighter shadow. It can then move in its orbit with its bright light, "borrowed" from the sun, no longer dimmed by the earth.

But, you may wonder, if this happens occasionally, why does it not happen every month? It does not because the moon's path is tilted (at a little more than five degrees) to the plane of the earth-sun orbit and, as a result, the moon usually passes above or below the earth's shadow.

But when it happens to be near the plane of the earth's orbit during full moon, an eclipse results.

Although eclipses do not take place at regular intervals, astronomers, having an understanding of the motions of sun, earth, and moon, can predict dates at which they will occur.

Besides lunar eclipses there are solar eclipses. As with a lunar eclipse, earth, sun, and moon must arrive at a certain relationship to each other to bring one about. A solar eclipse takes place when the moon gets between earth and sun.

Does it seem strange that the "little" moon (2,160 miles in diameter) can obscure the enormous sun (860,000 miles in diameter)? It is possible because although the sun is four hundred times larger, it is four hundred times farther from earth. So size and distance cancel each other, and to an observer on earth, sun and moon seem equal in size.

A total solar eclipse results when the moon's orbit crosses the earth-sun axis and the moon is in a direct line between earth and sun. Also the moon at the time must be close enough to the earth for the tip of its shadow to reach this planet. Then sunlight disappears; midday suddenly turns into a dark and eerie night.

The moon's shadow over the sun is not seen for long from any one place. Its path moves rapidly across the earth. The longest a total eclipse of the sun ever lasts in one area is seven minutes and forty seconds, and this maximum time is experienced only at the equator.

The path taken by a solar eclipse is called the "track" of the eclipse. It is about a hundred miles wide and three or four thousand miles long. Only from this limited area can an eclipse of the sun be seen.

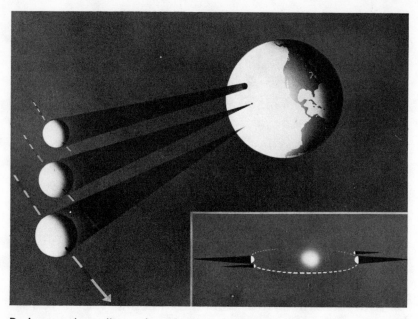

During a solar eclipse when the moon's shadow falls on the earth, the closeness of this satellite to the earth determines how large an area the eclipse will cover.

By contrast an eclipse of the moon, when the moon is above the horizon, may be seen at the same time from all parts of the earth; it is not limited to a narrow track. Lunar eclipses, however, are of no great interest to astronomers. But during an eclipse of the sun, astronomers are always excited about examining this great star, hoping to learn something about its mysteries. They travel around the earth to be at the right place at the right time to have the opportunity of observing a solar eclipse.

It is easy to list ways in which the sun affects the earth. In comparison it may seem the moon has no direct influence whatever on our planet. But one very obvious influence that we can see is the ebb and flow of tides.

THE MOON

9

Tides of Sea, Land, and Air

If you live near a seashore, or visit one for any length of time, you are sure to know something about tides. If you are interested in swimming and fishing, you soon learn when to expect high tide and low tide, and so can arrange your activities for a time when the height of the water on the shore is best for them.

In general there are two high and two low tides each day, with high tide and low occurring about six hours apart, and you probably can find a schedule of their arrivals in a local newspaper. But have you ever worked out your own timetable of tides by consulting the moon? This can be done because when the moon is overhead, the tide is high. As the moon moves in its orbit, the tidal bulge follows it (until it is stopped by a land mass), and by the time the moon has gone from sight, the tide is low.

Interestingly enough, high tides are created in the oceans on the opposite sides of the earth at the same time. This occurs because the moon's gravitational pull decreases as the distance from it increases. The water, therefore, in the oceans on the side opposite the moon's pull is attracted by the moon less than any other water on earth. But at the same time the motion of the earth's rotation and revolution tends to throw the water out into space, and the result is a high tide there also. High tides on the side of the earth facing the moon are called direct tides. High tides on the other side are called opposite tides.

With this evident connection, it would seem that people from earliest times would have recognized a relationship between the moon and tides. However, knowledge about the cause of tides was a long time in coming. For centuries explanations followed a pattern of strange myths and legends. One suggested the existence of a gigantic sea monster whose breathing, in and out, was strong enough to pull and push the waters of the ocean!

But eventually as people increasingly studied the heavens, they noted that the tides followed along with the moon's schedule. If the moon was rising about an hour later each day than the day before, the peak of the tide also occurred about an hour later than its peak the day before.

While this must have been interesting, especially to astronomers, there was still no explanation of the connection. That did not come until the law of gravity was discovered by Isaac Newton. This "natural law" dealing with the force of attraction between objects, was having its way with the earth, moon, and sun; and gravitation explained the "mystery" of tides.

Both the moon and the sun pull at everything on earth —rocks and mountains as well as water. However, rocks

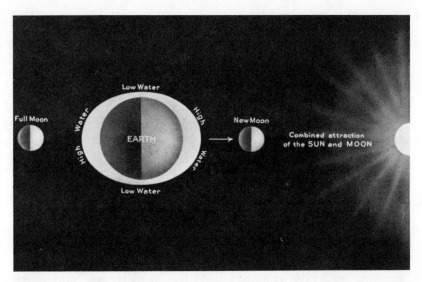

Tides are produced on earth by the gravitational pull of the moon, and "spring" tides (which have a greater than normal range) result when sun, moon, and earth are in a straight line so that the forces of moon and sun are combined.

and mountains are so strong and rigid we cannot see them move. Because water is fluid, the gravitational pull can lift it like a wave. In fact, this movement of water may be called a true tidal wave—a very different thing from a tidal wave caused by volcanic disturbances on a sea floor.

It might seem that the sun would have a greater pulling power because it is about 27 million times as large as the moon, but because it is so much farther away from the earth, the moon's pull is twice as strong.

Besides the daily changes in tides, four variations occur each month. There are two spring tides and two neap tides.

In this case the term "spring" is not connected with the season of the year; it is the name given to extra high tides, caused when earth, moon, and sun are in a straight line in the heavens. The gravitational pull of moon and sun are then combined. As a result, water on the earth is pulled up higher than during the rest of the month. This line-up of earth, moon, and sun takes place at the times of new moon and full moon.

Neap tides, by contrast, occur at first quarter and third quarter, when moon and sun are out of line, their positions, combined with that of the earth, making up the three points of a triangle. So, instead of their pulling together, they are to some extent offsetting each other's influence. This results in "high tides" that are lower than usual—the neap tides.

About twice a year when exceptionally high tides may be seen, we know that not only are sun, moon, and earth in a straight line, but the moon is as close to the earth as it ever comes during its elliptical orbit. Therefore its pull has extra power.

If you travel to widespread areas of the world, you may be puzzled by still further variations in tides. In the Bay of Fundy between Maine and Canada, twice a day billions of tons of water rush into the bay. During spring tides there the water may rise as much as fifty feet. On other shores, such as along the Gulf of Mexico and the Mediterranean Sea, tides rise no more than three or four feet when they are at their highest. Along Cape Cod, only a few hundred miles from the Bay of Fundy, tides rise little more than eight feet.

Several factors play a part in such variations. Very important is the topography of an area. At the Bay of Fundy the bay is very narrow. Its borders are so high that the water coming toward it in a swelling tide cannot spread out and instead it must rise. But along the Gulf of Mexico or other shores that are open and unrestricted,

The water was way up there! At the Bay of Fundy the difference between high and low tide is so great fishermen can work in an unusual way. They hang nets at high-tide height so that fish are trapped at that level. Then when the tide goes out, they climb up to collect. The high tides roll in twice a day.

the incoming waters can spread evenly across great stretches.

Another factor in regulating tides is the shape of the sea bottom. The floor of a great ocean is not regular in its contours. It has mountains and chasms that cut it up into many separate basins, and even though these divisions are far beneath the surface, they have a definite effect on the water's movements—including tides. Air pressures and high winds are other factors that contribute to the behavior of tides.

There are tides also in lakes and rivers.

While tides at a seashore are easily observed, the result of moon and sun pulling on solid earth is not. And you do not feel it because you stand on the earth and rise and fall with it. You are no more conscious of these movements than you are of the earth's rotation—because you are rotating with the earth. Nevertheless, instruments can measure the tides of solid bodies.

As with water, the extent of land tides varies with local conditions. In some areas the rise may be as much as twenty inches when the moon is directly overhead.

Because the atmosphere is made of gases, it is influenced even more strongly than water by the pull of the moon. Where a high tide is occurring in the ocean, an even higher tide is taking place in the atmosphere. But of course this is not visible to us.

10
Those Other Moons

Before 1610, the year Galileo discovered four of Jupiter's satellites far out in the solar system, the existence of any moon other than our own was a possibility ignored by most scientists, though it had been hinted at by such far-sighted men as the Polish astronomer Nicolaus Copernicus more than a hundred years before Galileo's time.

However, in the years that followed, the discovery of more and more moons forced astronomers to change their concepts of the pattern of the solar system.

In the 1800s many scientists felt that the satellite system of any planet was simply a scaled-down version of the solar system. But the twentieth century brought the discovery of a number of new satellites which, because of the irregularity of their orbits, contradicted such an orderly scheme.

For example, most members of the solar system revolve and rotate in a clockwise, or *prograde*, direction. This is not true of all moons however; some of them rotate in a

An artist interprets how Mars would appear from Phobos, the larger of its two moons and the one closest to it.

counterclockwise, or *retrograde,* motion around prograde-spinning planets. While the origin of these moons is uncertain, it seems fairly safe to state they must not have come directly from the planets they orbit, but were probably captured from space.

Two groups of Jupiter's outer satellites, one prograde and one retrograde, are good examples of this. They have such similar orbits that they are thought to be fragments resulting from a collision between a satellite of Jupiter and a stray piece of interplanetary matter in the process of being captured or nearly captured.

Recent photographs of the two Martian satellites, Phobos and Deimos, show moons irregular in shape and heavily cratered. This would seem to indicate a history in which fragmentation and collision with other bodies were involved. They may have been asteroids captured by Martian gravitation, or they may be fragments of an original, larger Martian satellite that was struck and broken apart by an asteroid.

The question that still remains unanswered is whether *all* satellites were originally interplanetary matter that was captured, or whether they were by-products of the formation of a parent planet.

The planets that orbit our sun differ in the number of satellites they control. Mercury and Venus have none. Possibly their closeness to the sun is the reason, because the force of gravity increases as the distance between objects decreases. Therefore, the sun could pull any potential satellites of Venus and Mercury into its fiery interior. Earth, of course, has its one moon—a moon, it is interesting to note, larger in relation to the planet it orbits than is any other satellite in the solar system. In fact, viewed from outer space, our planet and moon look more like a twin-planet system than a planet and its satellite.

Mars has two moons, both tiny compared with ours. Phobos, the larger of the two, is approximately 17 by 13½ by 12 miles. Deimos is about 9½ by 7½ by 7 miles. They are not round as our moon is. In fact, according to Dr. Carl Sagan of Cornell University, Phobos resembles a "diseased potato."

The planet beyond Mars is Jupiter. Jupiter is the largest planet in the solar system. It also is the planet with the greatest number of moons—fourteen in all. Its four largest—Ganymede, Callisto, Io, and Europa—are the so-called Galilean satellites that were discovered by Galileo. A startling fact is that Io has an atmosphere! This was revealed by a probe of the Pioneer 10 spacecraft in 1973. The atmosphere, however, is extremely thin—only one billionth of the atmospheric pressure of earth.

Io appears reddish-brown, and speculation is that it may be covered with crystals of sodium chloride (table salt). It is darker red at its poles and is enveloped in a yellowish glow which astronomers think may come from a form of sulfur.

Ganymede, the largest of Jupiter's satellites, is larger than the planet Mercury. Photographs from Pioneer 11 show it may have craters and seas similar to those of our own moon. While Ganymede's composition is still to be proved, it is almost certainly covered with a layer of ice.

Beyond Jupiter lies Saturn, second only to Jupiter in size. And it has the second largest number of moons—ten in all. Scientists have little information about most of these, but Titan, the largest, may be the most interesting and important moon in the entire solar system.

Titan, like Callisto and Ganymede which orbit Jupiter, is larger than the planet Mercury. But more important than size is the fact that it seems to have a reasonably

An interpretation of the earth and moon as they might be seen from Venus, showing how the two bodies could suggest a "double planet."

Saturn's rings, pictured in this painting, may have resulted from the disintegration of one of Saturn's moons, or they may be material that never consolidated into a moon.

dense atmosphere. Made up mostly of methane and hydrogen, its atmospheric pressure is probably at least one-tenth that of earth. Titan is believed by some scientists to have ammonia and water in its atmosphere, and these ingredients served as the building blocks for life on earth. It is conceivable that even though Titan is extremely cold, the possible presence of volcanoes could create enough warmth to begin the miraculous chain of life.

Little is known about the remaining seven moons of the solar system. Five of them belong to the planet Uranus, and two belong to Neptune. One of these is Triton, the fourth largest moon in the solar system. Neptune may have had three moons at one time; Pluto, the ninth and most distant planet, may have originated as an escaped satellite of Neptune.

Our knowledge of the thirty-four moons in the solar system is obviously incomplete. However, as studies continue, we steadily gain in understanding of these small but important celestial bodies and increase our knowledge of the entire solar system.

11

Man-made Satellites

There are satellites—and satellites. The moon, of course, is our earth's ever-intriguing natural satellite. And there are others in the solar system which, like our moon, exist without man's having had any part in their creation. But in recent years another kind of satellite has become an important factor in our desire to understand the universe and to handle our problems on earth better. These are the artificial satellites designed, constructed, and sent into orbit by people. Some are meant purely for research, others are equipped to do specialized work.

The very first of those created by man was Russia's Sputnik (the name meaning "satellite" in Russian), which was sent into orbit in October 1957. This was purely a research operation.

Until that time no one knew what nearby space (that is, space just outside the earth's atmosphere) consisted of, to say nothing of outer space. Sputnik served its purpose well in reporting on the amount of air resistance that would be met at very high altitudes. However, in its second objective—finding what kinds of radiation existed there—it was not so successful. It did report on radiation to some extent, but had it been put into a somewhat larger orbit, it would have made a tremendous discovery: the Van Allen magnetic belt. This was to be revealed the following year by Explorer 1, the first satellite created by the United States.

Launched in January 1958, it had an orbit more than twice as large as that of Sputnik 1. It also was intended to report on radiation, and at first there seemed nothing different about its messages. Detectors on the satellites, when struck by radiation, made a click that came back to earth sounding like the cluck of a chicken. This was heard through earphones and recorded on tape. For a while the clicks came as expected. Then they definitely increased in speed. Then, they stopped completely.

Listening scientists thought that something had gone wrong with the mechanism, even though other equipment on the satellite, reporting on temperatures, was still functioning. But in less than an hour the radiation clicks were back. Soon they fell silent again, and the "on again–off again" pattern was repeated a number of times. Before long those who were studying the sounds could feel sure that the radiation counter was silenced when Explorer went above six hundred miles in its elliptical orbit, and they noticed that when the clicks started up again, they came on very fast.

A professor of physics, Dr. James Van Allen, went to work on this mystery, having the thought that at certain times the counter might become overloaded by too much radiation bombardment and, as a result, would report nothing at all.

Dr. Van Allen's idea proved correct, and the discovery was made that there is an extraordinary amount of radiation in an area beginning about six hundred miles above the earth's atmosphere. And so, in the professor's honor, the area was named the Van Allen Belt. Later, through the reports of another satellite, Pioneer 1, scientists discovered how far out into space the Van Allen Belt went, and that there was more than one "belt." This was important to know for future exploration by astronauts; they would have to be protected from harmful radiation.

Two years after Explorer 1, a satellite called Tiros 1 took television cameras into orbit which made the first pictures of cloud formations moving across the earth. And ever since, satellites have been continuing this type of recording, flashing pictures to weather stations all over the earth. Hundreds of ground stations are equipped to receive such information.

Weather satellites are now dependable pilots for ships at sea. Each ship is able to pick up signals about one that is in trouble. When a distress signal is relayed from a satellite to ground stations, the information goes out to ships that can go to the rescue. Weather satellites also help in searching out icebergs.

Other satellites are devoted to helping with pollution control on earth. Pictures taken from far out in space can show exactly where pollution in rivers is being carried into the ocean, and it can be traced as it goes out into the ocean for many miles. Polluted air also shows up in satellite photos. And satellite pictures of reservoirs will show if these water-storage areas are filling up with dirt and sediment. Some satellites help with checking forest fires.

A number of satellites seek out natural resources on earth. By taking remarkably detailed pictures of surface formations, they can help direct geologists to such natural treasures as copper, iron, oil, and uranium.

Thanks to pictures taken from satellites, the making of maps of the earth has been revolutionized, because one such photograph can cover ten thousand square miles.

A tremendously useful kind of satellite that is now quite taken for granted by most people is used in communications. By means of communications satellites, radio and television signals can be flashed around the world and brought to receiving sets in private homes. The first experimental satellites in this field were very simple. They were like giant silver balloons, inflated to a hundred feet and more after they were out in space. When radio signals were beamed up to them, the signals were bounced off them and returned to earth at some far-distant point. Such was Echo 1, launched in 1960, and a larger Echo 2 in 1964.

In 1962 a much smaller satellite was put into orbit, but it was far more complicated. There was radio equipment aboard to receive signals. An electronic tube in the transmitter and transistors magnified the signals more than a million times before relaying them to the earth. This was Telstar 1. It took its power from the sun.

Telstar 1 worked well until it was damaged by radiation from the Van Allen Belt. Then came a more powerful Telstar 2. Soon afterward Intelsat (International Telecommunications Satellite Consortium) was formed. This represented a group of fourteen nations at first, but it was enlarged to more than eighty members.

The first project of the consortium was the satellite Intelsat 1, often called Early Bird 1. Launched in April 1965, it could handle 240 telephone connections between Europe and the United States at one time. It was fol-

One of the early communications satellites, sent into orbit in 1964. This was Echo II, a silver sphere that inflated to a 135-foot diameter. Radio signals beamed toward the giant "balloon" bounced off it and returned to earth.

lowed by Intelsat 2, 3, and 4, and these four satellites orbiting the earth can handle all worldwide communications. There are now three Intelsat 4's carrying voice and television communications all over the world. Each has a life expectancy of about seven years.

Perhaps the most dramatic of all artificial satellites is Skylab—the huge experimental space station that was

launched in May 1973. This was conceived as a first step toward making it possible for people to live and work in space stations. It was sent into orbit about 270 miles above the earth—on its own, without a crew aboard, but with plans for three astronauts to follow shortly after, dock with it, and enter it to begin studies.

This project was known to be challenging, but no one suspected how great the challenge would be. Shortly after Skylab's take-off, a strong wind caused by the craft's passage through the atmosphere shredded the aluminum panel which was to have been a protection from the sun. Without such protection, the temperatures in Skylab would be unbearable. It seemed the great space experiment was doomed before it had really begun.

However, extraordinary work by ground controllers and by astronauts saved the mission. The first crew, arriving at the satellite eleven days later, managed to put a protective cover over it. The second crew, arriving two months later, put a huge awning over that—and Skylab survived as an efficient space laboratory. A third crew lived and worked in it for eighty-four days.

With the scores of man-made satellites now circling the earth, it seems amazing that they do not get in each other's way. But their orbits are carefully planned and controlled by space scientists and engineers. When a height has been decided upon, a rocket is fired to carry the satellite to the proper distance, where it forms a high arc.

A modern global communications satellite, Intelsat 3, about to be sent into orbit—22,300 miles distant from the earth—by a launch vehicle in Florida. This launching took place in 1970.

When it has reached the height of the arc, it will have passed through the earth's atmosphere, and it turns so that it is horizontal to the earth's surface. Another rocket then fires, and this puts the satellite into orbit.

Man-made satellites played a large part in the success of the Apollo missions to the moon. Not only did they check out radiation and other conditions in outer space; the many photographs of the moon made by them enabled scientists to choose the best possible landing sites for the Apollo astronauts.

Not many years ago, when radio beams were being bounced off balloon-type satellites, a well-known scientist wrote that it was "unfortunate" the moon was 240,000 miles away from the earth, because if it were a mere ten per cent of that distance, he said, it would be a fine natural reflector for radio beams.

But fortunately the moon has stayed in its own orbit, while astronomers, engineers, and other scientists have created means for putting us in close touch with this heavenly body which now promises to be a steppingstone to more distant planets.

12

The Value of the Moon

Different people have different ideas about "value." Many decide on values according to how much something might be sold for; others feel that value lies in the beauty of an object, or in its usefulness.

On what basis, then, can the moon and its explorations be appraised? In recent times it has been considered from all these points of view. When a lively interest in its possibilities was aroused early in the twentieth century, a few dishonest schemers managed to make money out of it by setting up a real estate company that offered moon properties to the public at a dollar an acre. Thousands of eager purchasers sent in one or more dollars, for which they received a deed for land "in Copernicus Crater on the northeast quadrant of the moon," and rights to "fishing and winter sports" near the site purchased.

Perhaps these lunar-minded people at some time managed to have a look at their purchases through powerful telescopes, but that was surely as close as they ever got to them.

MOON IS ON SALE, ONLY $1 AN ACRE

Long Islander Doing Land-Office Business in Deeds to Crater Bottomland

By ROBERT K. PLUMB

Several lawyers in the city were scratching their heads last night in amazement over a new deal that has come to light in Long Island real estate.

There are plenty of deals in Long Island real estate, of course. But in the latest, a Long Islander is selling deeds to one-acre plots for $1. The deeds are to an acre in Copernicus Crater on the northeast quadrant of the moon. So far, there are reported to be 4,500 buyers.

For $1, here is what the lunar buyer gets:

¶A general quitclaim to an acre of good crater bottomland. The fine print disposes of the mineral rights (including uranium). It gives the buyer fishing and winter sports rights near the site he purchased.

¶A brochure describing the wonders of the moon as they are at present envisioned by the developer of the area. The brochure waxes enthusiastic in the time-honored manner of real estate promoters.

¶A map that shows the purchaser how he can see his land through a powerful telescope

Portion of a news article published in The New York Times in 1919 concerning the sale of pieces of the moon.

Today, when expeditions to the moon have been accomplished and future travel is a certainty, no one is talking about selling or buying. Instead this small planet is expected to serve mankind in a variety of ways. At present, although no great effort is being made by the government to build laboratories or to start a space colony there, remarkable ideas have been thought through, and plans worked on, to use the moon as a key to improved living conditions on earth.

It is expected that science in many fields will benefit from laboratories established on the moon. In medical research, doctors could study the effect of low gravity on various organs of the human body. They might be able to develop new medications as they work in an area completely free of bacteria. In the field of nutrition, experiments with crops in moon laboratories might lead to better ways of producing food on earth, largely by creating better fertilizers. Astronomers using the moon as a base would be able to study other celestial bodies more completely than before since there would be no atmosphere to dull their observations. Further study of lunar minerals and rocks may add significant knowledge to what is already known of the earth's composition. And there is a good possibility of being able to mine valuable minerals on the moon to bring back to earth. It is hoped, also, that by recording and analyzing moonquakes, more understanding will be achieved regarding earthquakes, and perhaps ways will be discovered to control these violent forces in the earth.

The accomplishments of moon-dwelling scientists would be enormously increased because each one would be working in co-operation with experts on earth, with information constantly relayed between earth and moon.

Among the most dramatic future happenings on the moon will be the building of bases for planetary expeditions and the construction of living quarters for workers. Large aircraft corporations have already proposed plans for a lunar base that are considered practical. Among them is the construction of prefabricated cylinder-shaped units which would be sent to the moon by rocket cargo ship. After landing, several could be fitted together for working and living establishments for a small group of people. Separate units would be used to shelter power generators and other equipment.

From such simple beginnings it is predicted a much more complicated lunar base can grow—one large enough to serve a hundred or more people. There are differences of opinion as to where such a colony should be located. One leans toward having it buried underground in a lunar crater. Another feels it should be out in the open, but protected by huge domes. Still another favors excavating the side of a mountain for the purpose.

Wherever the colony is located, its members would have various means of traveling that were not available to the Apollo astronauts. There would be different types of roving vehicles and trucks—some of them designed to manage the sides of steep craters as well as flat plains. One kind now suggested is a rocket-powered scooter which would enable its driver to soar over the moon's surface.

Engineers are already designing more efficient tools and equipment for moon use. As the Apollo astronauts discovered, working on the moon with tools can be rather confusing because they handle differently in the moon's weaker gravity. Some "old fashioned" earth tools have proved efficient, but some are being redesigned and new ones are being worked out. For instance there is a "plench"—combining pliers and a wrench. And there is a space hammer called a "spammer." This can be attached to the surface of the object to be pounded; then a hammer head automatically does the pounding. There is no need for the workman to swing his arm.

Thick coverings will be made for such instruments as telescopes and solar batteries to protect them from blazing heat and bombardment by flying cosmic material.

Of course workers on the moon will continue to need space suits when they are away from their homes and laboratories where good air is mechanically supplied. It is not likely that people will ever be able to breathe freely when outdoors.

A number of ideas are being directed toward creating

oxygen for enclosed areas. One would be the growing of various earth plants. Gardens set up in flower boxes under plastic domes, drawing light from the sun, could be one type of producer. Plants such as pumpkins that give out generous amounts of oxygen would be especially desirable. They could also serve as food. (And who would not enjoy a pie made of moon-grown pumpkin, baked in a solar-powered oven?)

It is possible, also, that oxygen could be extracted from rocks with equipment powered by a solar-cell electrical system. In fact, many aspects of solar energy—a source of energy desperately needed on a grand scale for the earth—could open up through experimentation on the moon.

Already a number of benefits have been derived from inventions that were developed because of needs in lunar work. They are not generally known because, for the most part, they are extremely technical. But we find, for instance, new devices to help crippled people walk, based on those created to make moon-walking possible. Also there are now instruments so tiny they can be swallowed, or injected into the bloodstream of a patient, and will then safely and accurately diagnose ailments.

Altogether the moon offers many prospects of finding ways to improve life on earth, besides serving as an outer-space service station and a launching site for expeditions of the future. Undoubtedly the eager desire of humans to understand the universe completely will continue; and it is to be hoped that the moon, acting as a way station for those trying to reach other worlds, will bring nations together rather than dividing them. The development of something so universal as our majestic satellite planet surely should serve to unite people. In this could lie the moon's greatest value.

Appendix:
Moon Facts in Brief

PIONEERS

The number of people involved in pioneer space exploration, including those at the Launch Center at Cape Canaveral, Florida, and Mission Control at Houston, Texas, is
far too great for all of them to be named here. However,
in the following list you will find the names and ranks of
the American space pioneers whose participation is described in this book.

PROJECT MERCURY   BLAST-OFF DATE

Navy Commander Alan B. Shepard, Jr.   May 5, 1961
Lieutenant Colonel John H. Glenn, Jr.
                                  February 20, 1962

Project Apollo

Apollo 1   (Destroyed by fire January, 1967)

Navy Lieutenant Commander Roger B. Chaffee
Air Force Lieutenant Colonel Virgil I. ("Gus") Grissom
Air Force Lieutenant Edward H. White

Apollo 8   December 21, 1968

Air Force Major William A. Anders
Air Force Colonel Frank Borman
Navy Captain James A. Lovell, Jr.

Apollo 10   May 18, 1969

Navy Commander Eugene A. Cernan
Air Force Colonel Thomas P. Stafford
Navy Commander John W. Young

Apollo 11   July 16, 1969

Air Force Lieutenant Colonel Edwin E. ("Buzz") Aldrin,
    Jr.
Test Pilot and Astronaut Neil A. Armstrong
Air Force Lieutenant Michael Collins

Apollo 12   November 14, 1969

Navy Commander Alan L. Bean
Navy Commander Charles ("Pete") Conrad, Jr.
Navy Commander Richard F. Gordon, Jr.

Apollo 13   April 11, 1970

Test Pilot and Astronaut Fred W. Haise, Jr.
Navy Captain James A. Lovell, Jr.
Test Pilot and Astronaut John L. Swigert, Jr.

Apollo 14   January 31, 1971

Navy Commander Edgar D. Mitchell
Air Force Major Stuart A. Roosa
Navy Captain Alan B. Shepard, Jr.

Apollo 15   June 26, 1971

Air Force Lieutenant Colonel James B. Irwin
Air Force Colonel David R. Scott
Air Force Major Alfred M. Worden

Apollo 16   April 16, 1972

Air Force Lieutenant Charles M. Duke, Jr.
Navy Lieutenant Commander Thomas K. Mattingly II
Navy Captain John W. Young

Apollo 17   December 7, 1972

Navy Captain Eugene A. Cernan
Navy Commander Ronald E. Evans
Scientist and Astronaut Harrison H. ("Jack") Schmitt

LANDING SITES

Following are the landing sites chosen for Apollo missions
and successfully reached:

Apollo 11   Sea of Tranquillity (Mare Tranquillitatis)
Apollo 12   Ocean of Storms (Oceanus Procellarum)
Apollo 14   Fra Mauro region
Apollo 15   Between Mount Hadley and the Apennine
     Mountain Range
Apollo 16   Descartes Highlands
Apollo 17   Taurus-Littrow Valley

Diameter   2,160 miles

Mass $\frac{1}{81}$ that of earth

Volume $\frac{1}{49}$ that of earth

Density   about $\frac{3}{5}$ that of earth

Surface gravity $\frac{1}{6}$ that of earth

Velocity of motion   2,287 miles per hour, or 3,350 feet per second

Distance from earth   252,710 greatest; 238,857 mean; 221,463 least

Revolution period   29 days 12 hours 44 minutes 2.8 seconds from new moon to new moon; 27 days 7 hours 43 minutes 11.5 seconds, actual revolution time around earth

Rotation period   27 days 7 hours 43 minutes 11.5 seconds

Glossary

Definitions of words found in this book, in terms of their relationship to the moon:

ANORTHOSITIC ROCK a group of rocks, believed to be the most abundant type on the moon; makes up the highlands

APOGEE point at which the moon is most distant from the earth

ASTEROIDS small "planets" which revolve around the sun, mainly between Mars and Jupiter

BASALT an igneous rock; material of the lunar "seas"

BRECCIA rock formed from particles of older rocks

COMMUNICATIONS SATELLITE an orbiting body which relays signals between communication stations

CRATER a pit on the moon (often miles in diameter, steep, and mountainous)

CRESCENT the moon when only a slice of lighted portion may be seen from earth

DIAMETER   the distance across a circle or sphere from one side to the other, through the center

EARTHSHINE   sunlight reflected by earth

ECLIPSE   the result of one body being blocked out by another

ELLIPSE   an oval; shape of the moon's orbit

GIBBOUS   rounder than half moon but less round than full moon

GRAVITATION   force of attraction that exists between all particles of matter everywhere in universe

HORIZON   the line at which earth and sky appear to meet

INERTIA, NEWTON'S "LAW" OF   a body in motion tends to remain in motion—or at rest tends to remain at rest—until acted on by an outside force

KEPLER'S LAWS OF PLANETARY MOTION   explanations of the movements of planets

"KREEP" NORITE   lunar rock, found in the highlands

LIQUID OXYGEN (LOX)   the normally gaseous element oxygen cooled to a temperature of between $-297°$ F and $-361°$ F

MARE (plural, MARIA)   dark areas of moon, result of lava flows

METEOR   any of small bodies (often remains of comets) traveling through space

ORBIT   the continuing, curving path of an object moving through space

PENUMBRA   the lighter part of a shadow

PERIGEE   point at which the moon is closest to the earth

PROPELLANT   any energy-yielding material used to propel a vehicle; it may be either liquid or solid in form

RADIATION   energy emitted by the sun, some forms of which are harmful

REVOLUTION   the movement of a satellite in orbit, as of

the moon around the earth or of the earth around the sun

ROTATION   the spinning of an object on its axis

SATELLITE   an object in space that is revolving around another body

SELENOLOGY   the study of the moon (Selene: Greek goddess of moon)

SOLAR WIND   the result of explosions on the sun which send out positively and negatively charged particles of gas

UMBRA   the cone-shaped shadow projected from a planet or satellite on the side opposite the sun

Index

Dragon, moon-eating, 6, 9
Duke, Charles, Jr., 49, 50
Dunite rock, 71

Eagle (lunar module), 31, 34, 36–37
Early Bird 1 (man-made satellite), 96
Earth
  chemical difference from moon, 16
  continental drift, 36
  distance from moon, 36
  effect of gravitational pull on moon
    orbiting, 74, 75–78
  line-up with sun and moon for spring
    tides, 83, 84
  maps, 96
  moon satellite, 1, 89, 93
  and moon in solar eclipse, 79
  and moon visibility, 73, 74
  orbiting, 22, 23, 25
  origin, 17
  rock dating, 70
  rotation rate, 36, 75
  and sun in lunar eclipse, 78
Earthquakes, 103
Earthshine, 78
Echo 1 (man-made satellite), 96
Echo 2 (man-made satellite), 96, 97
Eclipse
  lunar, 7, 76, 78–79
  solar, 79–80
Elements
  in moon rocks, 67
  rare earth (REE), 71
Endeavor (spacecraft), 45, 48
England, 9–10
Europa (Jupiter satellite), 90
Evans, Ronald, 51
Explorer 1 (man-made satellite), 94, 95

Falcon (lunar module), 45
Farming, 8, 9, 10
Ferropseudobrookite (mineral), 70
Fifth Lunar Science Conference, 17
Fines rock group, 67
First Men in the Moon, The, 18
Fishing, 8, 85
Food, space flight, 27
Fra Mauro moon area, 42, 43
Frog, moon-eating, 7
From the Earth to the Moon, 18

Gabbro volcanic rock, 55, 68
Gagarin, Yuri, 22
Galilean satellites, 90
Galileo, 2, 54–55, 87, 90
Ganymede (Jupiter satellite), 90
Gault, Donald, 58
Gemini docking missions, 23, 25, 27
Genesis rock, 71
Geologists, 51, 96
Geology, 51
  and moon rock testing, 65, 67
Ghost craters, 57

Glenn, John, Jr., 23
Glove boxes, 65
Goddard, Robert H., 19, 20
Gold, 16
Gordon, Richard, Jr., 38
Gravitational pull
  combined moon and sun, 84
  of earth, 74, 75–78
  of moon, 82, 83, 84
  of sun, 15, 81
Gravity, 18, 82
  balance with inertia, 77–78
Grissom, Virgil, 26
Gulf of Mexico tides, 84

Hadley-Apennine moon area, 71
Hadley Rille, 45, 47, 55, 60
Haise, Fred, Jr., 42
Ham (chimpanzee), 22
Harvest moon, 9
Herschel, John, 11–12

Igneous rocks, 67, 70
Ilmenite, 70
Inertia, balance with gravity, 77–78
Intelsat (International
    Telecommunications Satellite
    Consortium), 96–97, 99
Interplanetary matter, 89
Intrepid (lunar module), 39, 40, 41
Io (Jupiter satellite), 90
Iron, 16, 68, 70, 71, 96
Iroquois Indians, moon legends, 7
Irwin, James, 45, 46, 48

Jack and Jill rhyme, 10–11
Jupiter (planet), 1, 2, 16, 87
  satellites, 89, 90

K (potassium), 71
Kitty Hawk (spacecraft), 43, 44
Komarov, Vladimir, 26
KREEP, 71
Kuiper, Gerard P., 15–16

Lake of Dreams, 55
Laser beam mirror, 36
Lava, 55, 70, 71
Littrow moon crater, 51
Locke, Richard, 12–13
Lovell, James, 28, 42
Luck, 11
Lunar eclipse, 7, 76, 78–79
Lunar module (LM), 23, 30, 31, 39, 40,
    42, 45, 46, 48
Lunar phases, 8, 9, 10, 74–75
Lunar Receiving Laboratory, 65
Lunar rocks. *See* Moon rocks
Lunar rover (LR), 45, 46, 47, 48, 50, 52,
    63
Lunar Sample Analysis team, 69

Pyroxmanganite, 70

Radiation research, 94–95
Radiometric dating, 69–70
Radio signals, 97, 100
Ranger rockets, 23, 25
  Ranger 7, 23–24, 61
  Ranger 8, 24
Rare earth elements (REE), 71
Ray craters, 59
Reaping, 9
Redstone (rocket), 23
Regolith (lunar soil), 60, 67
Resonance theory, 15
Rilles, 45, 56, 60
Ringed plains, 59
Rockets and rocketing, 19–29
Roosa, Stuart, 43, 44
Russia, rocketing program, 19, 21, 93–94

Sagan, Carl, 90
Satellites, man-made, 21–22, 23, 93–100
Satellites, planets', 1–2, 77, 87–92
  Galilean, 90
Saturn (planet), 1, 16, 90, 91
Saturn V (rocket), 25
Scandinavia, moon legends, 10
Schmitt, Jack, 51, 52, 63
Scott, David, 45, 48
Sea of Clouds, 24, 56
Sea of Crises, 48
Sea of Tranquillity, 24, 31, 48, 55, 69, 70
Seas, moon, 54–55, 57, 71
Seismometer, 35, 36, 41, 64
Shepard, Alan, Jr., 22–23, 43, 44
Shipping, 95
Silicone, 71
Skylab, 5, 97–100
Skylab Student Project, 5
Smithsonian Institution, 3
Snoopy (lunar module), 30
Solar eclipse, 79–80
Solar energy, 105
Solar system, 15–16
  clockwise (prograde) rotation, 87
  counterclockwise (retrograde) rotation, 88
  moons (satellites) in, 1–2, 77, 87–92
Solar-wind experiments, 36, 66
Space Age, 5, 12
Spacecraft, 22–23
Space Suits, 37, 40, 45, 104
Space walks, 23
Spammer, 104
Splash-down, 29
Spring tides, 83, 84
Sputniks, 21, 22, 93–94
Stafford, Thomas, 29, 30
Sun
  and earth in lunar eclipse, 78
  eclipse of, 79–80

gravitational pull on earth, 15
line-up with moon and earth for spring tides, 83, 84
and moon legends, 9
and moon visibility, 73, 74
orbiting, 89
Sun Goddess, 8
Surveyor 3 (rocket), 38, 40, 41
Swigert, John, Jr., 42

Taurus moon area, 51
Taurus-Littrow valley, 33, 51, 63, 71
Telephone, and satellites, 96–97
Television, and satellites, 95, 97
Telstar 1 and 2 satellites, 96
Through the Looking Glass and What Alice Found There, 72
Tidal wave, 83
Tides, 7–8, 14, 81–86
  direct, 82
  high, 81–82, 84, 85
  low, 81
  neap, 83, 84
  opposite, 82
  spring, 83, 84
Tiros 1 (man-made satellite), 95
Titan (Saturn satellite), 90, 92
Titanium, 67
Tranquillity Base, 31
Triton (Neptune satellite), 92
Troilite, 70
Tycho crater, 59

Umbra, 78
Uranium, 16, 70, 96
Uranus (planet), 1, 92
U. S. Geological Survey, 50, 51

Van Allen, James, 94–95
Van Allen magnetic belt, 94, 95, 96
Venus (planet), 88, 89
Verne, Jules, 18
Viking-Mars program, 5
Viking rockets, 20
Volcanism, 55, 56, 64, 71
V-2 rocket, 19, 20

Walled plains, 59
Weather satellites, 95
Weightlessness, 18
Wells, H. G., 18
White, Edward, 26
White Sands proving ground, 19–20
Worden, Alfred, 45
World War II, 19

Yankee Clipper (spacecraft), 38, 39, 41
Young, John, 29, 49, 50
Yttrium, 67

Zirconium, 67

About the Authors

DOROTHY E. SHUTTLESWORTH has taken an interest in natural sciences and conservation since she began working at the American Museum of Natural History in New York at the age of seventeen. There she was editor of *Junior Natural History Magazine* for a dozen years, during which time she began writing books for young people. Her family includes her husband, Melvin Shuttlesworth; a son, Gregory, who is an energy specialist with an international consulting firm; and a daughter, Lee Ann, who coauthored *The Moon* with her mother. Mrs. Shuttlesworth is one of the founders of New Jersey Citizens for Clean Air, Inc.

LEE ANN WILLIAMS received a B.S. degree from the University of Kentucky, and is now teaching science at the Intermediate School of Maywood, New Jersey.

		DATE DUE	
~~Smith J~~	JAN. 3		
Felicia S.	AP 08 '85		

```
523.3      Shuttlesworth,
Shuttles- Dorothy E
 worth    Moon, stepping
          stone to outer
```